"After saving us with heroic sandwiches and baking up wholesome, vegan baked goods in their previous books, Tami and Celine nourish vegans once again with their latest batch of protein-rich recipes."
—Terry Hope Romero, author of *Veganomicon*, *Salad Samurai*, and more

"I thought that I had thorough knowledge of vegan proteins, but after reading Celine and Tami's book, I've learned so much more. No one needs to worry about incorporating delicious, protein-filled vegan food into their diet while this book exists!"
—Jackie Sobon, founder of Vegan Yack Attack (veganyackattack.com)

"Tami and Celine prove once and for all that vegan diets can be full of protein-rich foods. *The Great Vegan Protein Book* is full of so many delicious and creative protein-rich recipes that the question should no longer be, 'Where do you get your protein?' but rather, 'Where *don't* you get your protein?'"
—Dianne Wenz, vegan health and lifestyle coach (veggiegirl.com)

"One of the most frequent questions vegans are asked is, 'Where do you get quality protein sources?' Most people generally don't understand how protein rich plants can be. Even more confusing are outdated nutrition materials regarding combining food to get the proper amounts of protein from different vegan foods. Tamasin and Celine clear up these myths and show you just how easy and tasty it is to meet the FDA guideline of 50 grams or more of protein per day for adults entirely with plant-based foods in *The Great Vegan Protein Book*."
—Somer McCowan, blogger (www.vedgedout.com)

"Ever wonder where vegans get their protein? Tami and Celine have the answer and about 100 other delicious answers for you, too. This is a book you will definitely want in your cookbook library."
—Jason Wyrick, executive chef of The Vegan Taste and author of *Vegan Tacos*

*With many thanks to vegan cookbook testers everywhere,
and especially to those who have tested our books.
Without you sharing your time, energy, grocery budget,
and feedback, these recipes wouldn't see the light of day.*

First published in the USA in 2015 by
Fair Winds Press, a member of
Quarto Publishing Group USA Inc.
100 Cummings Center
Suite 406-L
Beverly, MA 01915-6101
www.fairwindspress.com

19 18 17 16 15   1 2 3 4 5

ISBN: 978-1-59233-643-2

Digital edition published in 2015
eISBN: 978-1-62788-187-6

Library of Congress Cataloging-in-Publication Data available

Book and cover design by *tabula rasa* graphic design
Photography by Celine Steen (www.celinesteen.com)
Nutrition review by Anya Todd, RD, LD (www.anyatodd.com)

Printed and bound in China

*The information in this book is for educational purposes only. It is not
intended to replace the advice of a physician or medical practitioner. Please
see your health care provider before beginning any new health program.*

THE GREAT VEGAN
PROTEIN
BOOK

Fill Up the Healthy Way with More Than
100 Delicious, Protein-Based Vegan Recipes

CELINE STEEN & TAMASIN NOYES

Fair Winds Press
100 Cummings Center, Suite 406L
Beverly, MA 01915

fairwindspress.com • quarryspoon.com

CONTENTS

"BUT WHERE WILL YOU GET YOUR PROTEIN?"

Putting This Recurring Vegan Question to Rest, Once and For All

If you've ever even considered going vegan, one of the first things you might have heard from well-meaning folks is, "But where will you get your protein?"

It seems that no one gives much thought to anyone else's protein intake until the moment you vaguely mention adopting a vegan life-style. After getting asked the "big question" so many times, we decided to write this book so everyone would be able to spout off loads of flavorful, satisfying, protein-packed recipes in one fell swoop (er, book).

We'll take a closer look at some of the most common sources of protein that are popular with both herbivores and omnivores alike, such as beans and grains, as well as some sources that may be new to you, such as seitan. We'll also demonstrate that there's no deprivation of *any kind* involved in going vegan. And, of course, we'll share creative and mouthwatering recipes that are packed with both protein and flavor! But to start off, let's answer a few of the most frequently asked questions that come up when people start talking about plant-based diets in general and protein in particular.

PLANT-BASED PROTEIN FAQ

You probably have a ton of questions. Protein can be a tricky issue, and we're going to try to simplify it so that you'll have a better understanding both for yourself and for those previously mentioned folks with good intentions. Best of all, you'll see that getting enough protein from a plant-based diet is easier than many people think.

It's vital to note, however, that if you have serious concerns or questions, you should consult with your doctor or a registered dietitian. Bodies aren't all identical, and nobody knows your body better than you do.

Why Do We Need Protein?

Protein is what makes our bodies work! We use it to build cells and maintain our bodies' systems. Our organs, bones, blood, muscles, and skin all require protein. It is also the building block of neurotransmitters, the messaging cells in our bodies that allow all of our systems to work and interrelate. These neurotransmitters are made of—you guessed it—protein. Our very DNA is made from protein, in fact, and so are all the cells in our bodies. As our cells die off and need to rebuild, our bodies use protein to complete that necessary process.

> "While most plant-based foods are not complete proteins, it's easy to get all the necessary amino acids we need from plants while following a balanced vegan diet."

To be even more precise, our bodies need the *amino acids* found in protein. There are twenty amino acids, eleven of which are manufactured by our bodies. The remaining nine come directly from food. While most foods contain amino acids, those found in *protein-rich* foods are the most usable. When we consume such foods, our systems break the protein down into the component amino acids. Then our bodies magically restructure the amino acids into the different patterns we need to address the various needs of our bodies. In short, we need protein for all of our physical functions.

Is Plant-Based Protein as Efficient as Animal Protein?

Animal-based proteins contain all nine amino acids in the perfect proportion for human bodies, making them *complete proteins* (which we'll explain more as follows). The downside is that animal-based proteins are often also high in cholesterol and saturated fats, which can be detrimental to our health and well-being.

While most plant-based foods are not complete proteins, it's easy to get all the amino acids we need from plants while following a balanced vegan diet. In fact, it can be *better* for you because plant-based proteins are naturally cholesterol-free, lower in heart-harming saturated fats, and contain more health-ful antioxidants and fiber than animal protein.

How Much Protein Does a Body Need?

Here's where it gets a little complicated because views and studies on this issue vary. The World Health Organization (WHO) recommends 10 to 15 per-cent of our diet be protein. The United States Department of Agriculture (USDA), on the other hand, presupposes that we eat an animal-based diet and recommends that 10 to 35 percent of our diet should be made of protein. Other studies indicate that we need significantly less protein to maintain a healthy diet. For example, the highly esteemed (and vegan) expert T. Colin Campbell, a respected nutritional biochemist, suggests that our diets should be 8 to 10 percent protein.

Choosing what protein intake works for you is a personal decision. If you'd like to calculate your specific protein needs in grams, the WHO suggests the following method:

(Your ideal weight in pounds) × 0.36 = daily protein intake in grams

Or

(Your ideal weight in kilograms) × 0.8 = daily protein intake in grams

Children, athletes, elderly people, and women at various times during their lives all have specific—and unique—protein needs. Let us emphasize the impor-tance of speaking with your doctor or a registered dietitian. Getting enough protein is easy, but information is vital.

What Is the Difference Between a Complete Protein and an Incomplete Protein?

A complete protein contains all nine essential amino acids in the most usable ratio that you need to consume for your body to function at its best. While an incomplete protein also contains those same amino acids, they are not in the same optimal ratio.

> "The important thing to remember is that it's best to get your protein intake from various sources throughout the day and to not overdo it with one single source."

Sure, animal-based proteins are complete proteins, but so are several vegan foods, such as soy foods, seitan, amaranth, and quinoa. And don't underestimate those incomplete proteins! Grains, beans, vegetables, and nuts are important, healthful options that will also help keep you going strong.

For years, the common belief was that proper nutrition required each meal to include a source of complete protein, either from a single complete-protein dish or a combination of two or more incomplete protein foods. Interestingly, many cultures have naturally combined foods in this manner for a long time. Beans and grains, which are typically eaten together in many cultures, are an example of combining foods to create a complete protein. Neither food has the right proportion of essential amino acids on its own, but they become a complete protein when eaten together—or even separately, if consumed within a 24-hour period, as new research now concludes is sufficient.

The fact is that as long as you consume a *variety* of protein-rich plant-based foods within a 24-hour period, your body will do just fine building complete proteins. We're putting the emphasis on eating a *varied* diet here, which is key to leading a healthy life and not only when it comes to protein intake.

Where Can I Find More Information on Protein?

As more people grow interested in veganism, there is an increasing number of wonderfully informative books on vegan nutrition as a whole. Here are a few of our favorites:

Vegan for Life by Jack Norris, R.D. and Virginia Messina, M.P.H., R.D. Da Capo Publishing, 2011.

The China Study by T. Colin Campbell, Ph.D. and Thomas M. Campbell II, M.D. BenBella Books, 2006.

Forks over Knives by Gene Stone, editor. The Experiment, 2011.

PLANT-BASED PROTEINS: AN OVERVIEW

The information that follows is further proof that the vegan world is seriously not lacking for choice in the protein-rich department. It almost makes one wonder where the idea of deprivation came from!

The important thing to remember is that it's best to get your protein intake from various sources throughout the day and to not overdo it with one single source. Just like you wouldn't (or shouldn't) have eaten the same plate of eggs or meat three times a day back when you weren't vegan, it would quickly become boring if you were to eat nothing but beans or tofu all the time—and this is where the 100+ recipes in this book come in handy!

Beans and Legumes

With all the fiber and protein contained in beans, lentils, and peas, it's no wonder that these nutritional powerhouses are the number one source of protein that pops into mind when the subject of veganism comes up. A 1-cup (weight will vary) portion of most cooked beans, lentils, and peas offers approximately 15 to 18 g of protein. (See the chart on page 17.)

Beans are available both dry and canned. It's up to you to decide what option you like best: cooking big batches of beans yourself or the convenience of having them ready to use as canned. One average 15-ounce (425 g) can contains approximately 1½ cups (weight will vary) of beans. If using canned, be sure to drain the liquid and rinse the beans thoroughly until the water runs clear so that the beans can be easily digested and the excess sodium is washed away.

If you choose to do the cooking yourself, you will need to soak the rinsed and picked-through beans in cold water to a 1:3 ratio for approximately 6 hours (or overnight) before cooking. Drain the liquid, rinse the beans, and cook in fresh water for 1 to 1½ hours or until tender. As a general rule, dry beans will yield approximately three times their amount once cooked, so if you're economical and have the time, this is the way to go!

If you don't have time for the long soak, but still want to use dried beans, you can go for the quicker solution. Add the rinsed and picked-through beans to cold water in a large pot and then bring them to a boil. Remove the pot from the heat, cover with a lid, and let them soak for 1 to 2 hours. Drain the liquid, rinse the beans, and cook in fresh water for 1 to 1½ hours or until tender.

Note that you shouldn't add salt or any acidic ingredient to the beans while they are cooking as it can hinder the cooking process. Only proceed with these additions once the beans are tender.

Lentils and peas do not require any soaking prior to being cooked, which makes them ideal for fiber-rich, protein-packed, filling meals that are quick to land on the table. Just rinse and pick them through, drain well, add to boiling water, and cook for 25 to 45 minutes (or follow the instructions on the package).

Grains

Grains are packed with great overall nutrition as well as fiber to stave off hunger and improve digestion. They're also an excellent source of protein. Indeed, a 3.5-ounce (100 g) portion of cooked whole grains contains anywhere between 3 and 13 g of protein, depending on the grain. (See the chart on page 17.)

> "When properly stored in an airtight container in the refrigerator, cooked grains can last at least a week, making for quick meals on busy weeknights."

We should note that refined grains lose a massive amount of that wonderful nutritional value: Once the bran and germ are removed, about 25 percent of the grain's protein content is lost as well. In order to get all the goodness nature offers us, it's ideal to enjoy unrefined whole grains as often as possible. But it doesn't have to be all or nothing: There's absolutely nothing wrong with enjoying refined grains when the mood strikes you. It's all about balance.

Just like beans and legumes, most grains need to be picked through for debris straight out of the package and rinsed thoroughly in a fine-mesh sieve; make that a really, really fine-mesh sieve in the case of tiny amaranth seeds.

If you prefer your grains al dente like we do and find that the instructions included on most packages don't mesh with your preference, adjust the amount of liquid and cooking time accordingly. Cooking times vary depending on the freshness of the grain, and even on the cooking implements used, so keep an eye on the grain as it cooks and follow your own textural preference for doneness. It's far preferable to have to drain a little extra liquid, rather than have to put up with mushiness. Or, conversely, to add a little extra liquid and continue cooking if the grain isn't tender enough for your taste.

In order to create or boost any dish in a snap, we recommend having your favorite grains cooked and at the ready in the refrigerator or freezer. When properly stored in an airtight container in the refrigerator, cooked grains can last at least a week, making for quick meals on busy weeknights. For freezing, add the cooked grains to a large freezer bag, push out excess air and seal, and then lay flat and freeze on top of a cookie sheet (this makes for easy stacking once frozen). Crack off portions as needed (this works best when your layer of frozen grain is relatively thin) or run the bag under warm water to quickly defrost.

To maintain freshness, be sure to store all your dry grains and flours in airtight containers. Flours made from whole grains may also be stored in the freezer to keep them from going rancid.

LESSER KNOWN GRAINS

We understand not everyone is familiar with grains like amaranth and freekeh, so here is a quick little introduction. You'll see them featured in a few of our recipes (such as the Crispy Amaranth Patties on page 88 and the Broccoli and Mushroom Freekehzotto on page 90), so we want you to be prepared!

Amaranth: Originally from Peru, amaranth is actually a gluten-free pseudocereal (a different plant species that produces *seeds*, which are treated like grains). Pseudocereals have a nutritional profile that makes them quite similar to actual grains even though they aren't, botanically-speaking. Amaranth is a complete source of protein. Cooked amaranth has a mildly nutty taste and contains 4 g of protein per 3.5-ounce (100 g) portion. It absorbs other flavors very well, making it great in porridges, patties, and soups.

Farro: Highly popular in ancient Rome and considered to be the elder of all types of wheat, this hearty grain has a pleasantly nutty flavor. A 3.5-ounce (100 g) portion boasts approximately 7 grams of protein. We love to use the quick-cooking kind, but regular farro is perfect too—it'll just take an extra 15 to 20 minutes to cook, rather than the 10 minutes the quick-cooking kind calls for.

Freekeh: Freekeh is an ancient grain from the Middle East which is made from young green wheat, making it more vitamin- and mineral-dense than mature wheat. A 3.5-ounce (100 g) portion contains nearly 13 grams of protein. It is also packed with fiber—about 17 grams! Freekeh is available whole (which looks like wheat berries) or in cracked form, which is just that. The cracked is quicker-cooking and very convenient. However, we prefer whole and use it for pilafs, salads, soups, or as a simple side dish, among other things. While popular throughout the world, freekeh is just catching on in the United States. Look for it in well-stocked grocery stores, natural food stores, or online.

Nuts and Seeds

The fact that nuts and seeds are loaded with protein only makes them more of an irresistible snack! Most nuts and seeds contain anywhere between 3 and 9 g of protein per 1-ounce (28 g) serving, as well as a fair amount of fiber and omega-3 fatty acids, which makes them an ideal snack choice for curbing hunger the healthy way. Their main disadvantage, however, is their fat and calorie content: As with all good things, enjoying nuts and seeds in moderation is the way to go.

"Most nuts and seeds contain anywhere between 3 and 9 g of protein per 1-ounce (28 g) serving as well as a fair amount of fiber and omega-3 fatty acids, which make them an ideal snack choice for curbing hunger the healthy way."

And remember, the more naked the nuts and seeds, the better. Once they're coated with oil, corn syrup, and other stuff you can't pronounce, their nutritional value decreases rapidly. (Seriously, just look at a "flavored" type at your grocery store.) Munch on a small handful of plain, dry-roasted almonds instead, and you'll see that there's not much required to make nuts taste outstanding.

The same *au naturel* idea applies to the nut butters and spreads created from those nuts and seeds: the simpler the spread, the better. That's why we choose natural (sometimes called "old-fashioned") nut and seed butters over those loaded with sugar and other unnecessary fillers. Natural nut and seed butters need to be stirred before use, as their oils will separate. Those butters, and all whole nuts and seeds as a matter of fact, should be stored in the refrigerator to keep them from going rancid.

CHIA SEEDS

Nutrient-dense chia seeds are rich in omega fatty acids and contain 3 g of protein (and 5 g of fiber!) per tablespoon (12 g). The seeds expand when added to liquid, which makes them ideal for puddings. Both white and black chia seeds are available in most markets; their main difference lies mostly in what they're used for. In light-colored puddings or cakes, it is preferable to use white chia seeds because they will be less noticeable. Otherwise, slightly cheaper and easier-to-find black chia seeds can be used in things like bread, crackers, and so on.

HEMP SEEDS

Three tablespoons (30 g) of nutty-flavored, omegas-rich shelled hemp seeds contain 10 g of protein. They are a bit on the costly side, but their nutritional profile makes them more than worthy of being added to one's diet. We also like using them in the form of powder, as we do in our Mushroom Cashew Mini Pies (page 84) and Do The Cocoa Shake (page 88).

QUINOA

As a seed that is both a complete protein and gluten-free to boot, it took no time for quinoa to take the vegan (and nonvegan) world by storm. Often treated and cooked like a grain even though it isn't (botanically-speaking), cooked quinoa contains 4 g of protein per 3.5-ounce (100 g) portion.

One cup (173 g) of dry quinoa yields approximately 3 cups (555 g) cooked. Quinoa needs to be cooked in water or vegetable broth in a 2:1 water to quinoa ratio, although some people (ourselves included) like it to retain a little more texture and go for a 1¾:1 ratio of water to quinoa instead. To get the best results, it is necessary to thoroughly rinse your quinoa in a fine-mesh sieve to get rid of the saponin, which coats the seeds and gives quinoa a bitter taste if not rinsed out.

For extra flavor, you can toast the rinsed and thoroughly drained quinoa by drizzling a little oil in a saucepan, adding the quinoa, and cooking it on medium-high heat for about 1 minute or until the quinoa becomes fragrant. (This toasting method works for most whole grains, by the way.)

After that, all you need to do is add the liquid, stir well, and bring to a boil. Once the boiling starts, lower the heat to a low simmer and cover with a lid. Cook between 12 and 15 minutes until the liquid is absorbed. Remove from the heat and let stand 5 minutes. Remove the lid, fluff with a fork, and enjoy.

Seitan (a.k.a. Wheat Meat)

Sometimes seitan is called a "mock meat," which rubs us the wrong way. It's been popular with Buddhist monks in China and Japan for at least 1,000 years, so we think it's more than earned its place as a true food. Interestingly, the Japanese *sei* in English means "made of" while *tan* means "protein."

Traditionally, seitan is made from wheat flour, which is kneaded and rinsed many times, and then gently simmered in broth. Now, it's more common to start with vital wheat gluten, sometimes adding flours and seasonings to enhance its taste and vary the texture.

Seitan is a very efficient complete protein: one 3.5-ounce (100 g) serving contains about 16 g of protein.

Raw seitan can be steamed, simmered on the stove top or in a slow cooker, baked in the oven, or a combination of any of these; different methods result in different textures. Typically, once the seitan has been cooked in some way, it is ready to be used in a recipe.

If you prefer to buy premade seitan, it is usually available in the refrigerated section of natural food stores. But given how easy (and how much tastier!) homemade is, we encourage you to make your own. Be sure to see our recipes for Kind-to-Cows Seitan (page 138) and Quit-the-Cluck Seitan (page 138).

Tofu and Tempeh

Although both tofu and tempeh are made from soybeans, there are many differences between the two. Let's start first with tofu.

Originating more than 2,000 years ago in China, tofu is made from coagulated soymilk and is available in the refrigerated section of grocery stores. Tofu is packed with protein: an average ½ cup (126 g) serving of tofu has 10 grams of protein. For an even higher protein content, look for "sprouted tofu," which has nearly twice as much protein, but is also higher in calories, fat, and sodium.

We generally use the silken (in various stages of firmness), extra-firm, or super firm types, as will be noted in our recipes. Please do not use silken tofu unless it is specifically called for in a recipe, as the outcome will be quite different.

Silken and super firm types of tofu don't need to be pressed (just quickly drained), but other varieties do in order to get the most flavorful results. This is done by draining the tofu, then wrapping it in paper towels or tea towels, and placing a weight such as a cutting board on top. Tofu should be pressed for at least one hour. For longer pressing, put the tofu in the refrigerator, changing the paper towels occasionally as they become saturated with liquid. Commercial devices, such as the TofuXpress, are also highly effective and available online.

Tempeh is a fermented food that first appeared on the scene in the early 1800s in Indonesia. It is made from cracked, partially cooked soybeans. A tempeh starter (technically a fungus) is introduced and the bean mixture is formed into cakes and placed in an incubator for 2 to 4 days. During this time, fermentation occurs and solidifies the tempeh cake. While the process may sound a little strange, trust us: The taste of tempeh is sensational when properly prepared. We like to simmer it in boiling water for 20 minutes, and then drain and cut it into pieces before using in our recipes.

While tofu certainly carries its weight in the protein department, tempeh is even more protein-dense. A 4-ounce (115 g) serving contains approximately 21 g of protein (depending on the brand). Some people find tempeh to be easier to digest than tofu, too. Both tofu and tempeh are complete proteins on their own.

Nutritional Yeast
Nutritional yeast is a deactivated yeast (*i.e.,* it has no leavening power). It is packed with B vitamins and protein: a mere 2 tablespoons (15 g) contains 8 g of protein. Not to be confused with brewer's yeast, nutritional yeast is yellow and tastes savory as well as slightly cheesy. We strongly recommend the Red Star brand, as not all brands contain vitamin B12.

Nutritional yeast comes in various sizes of flakes, which makes its weight vary depending on the brand and whether it's bought in bulk. We get ours in bulk, and the flakes look almost powder-like. If you can only find large flakes, pulse them a few times in a food processor before measuring to get the best results.

Vegetables
If you thought all vegetables do is provide us with vitamins and fiber, think again: They also take pretty great care of us on the protein front. Potatoes, mushrooms, broccoli, Brussels sprouts, carrots, cauliflower, corn, kale, and more all contain between 2 and 5 g of protein per cup (weight will vary). All the more reason to do as Mom said and "Eat your vegetables!"

A FEW LESS COMMON KITCHEN INGREDIENTS
We always do our best to cook with well-known and readily available ingredients, but there might be a few that aren't familiar to you. If you aren't able to find some of these items at a well-stocked grocery store or natural food store, consider ordering them online.

Bouillon: Bouillon is a quick and easy way to add flavor to a dish and an instant way to make soup broth. It's concentrated and comes in either paste, powder, or cube form. One of the bouillons we use most frequently is a paste made by a brand called Superior Touch. For a vegetable base (such as in our Shorba, page 31), we use Better than Bouillon Vegetable Base and for a chicken-style

VEGAN PROTEIN SOURCES

PLANT-BASED FOOD	PROTEIN PER SERVING
Almonds (1 ounce, or 28 g)	6 g
Almond butter (2 tablespoons, or 32 g)	7 g
Amaranth, cooked (3.5 ounces, or 100 g)	4 g
Black beans, cooked (1 cup, or 172 g)	15 g
Black-eyed peas, cooked (1 cup, or 171 g)	13 g
Broccoli, cooked (1 cup, or 156 g)	4 g
Brown rice, cooked (3.5 ounces, or 100 g)	3 g
Brussels sprouts, cooked (1 cup, or 156 g)	4 g
Cannellini beans, cooked (1 cup, or 177 g)	17 g
Cashews (1 ounce, or 28 g)	5 g
Chia seeds (1 tablespoon, or 12 g)	3 g
Chickpeas, cooked (1 cup, or 164 g)	15 g
Edamame, cooked (1 cup, or 155 g)	17 g
Farro, cooked (3.5 ounces, or 100 g)	7 g
Flaxseeds (2 tablespoons, or 15 g)	3 g
Freekeh, whole, cooked (3.5 ounces, or 100 g)	13 g
Green peas, cooked (1 cup, or 160 g)	9 g
Hemp seeds, shelled (3 tablespoons, or 30 g)	10 g
Kale (1 cup, or 67 g)	3 g
Lentils, cooked (1 cup, or 198 g)	18 g
Nutritional yeast (2 tablespoons, or 15 g)	8 g
Peanuts (1 ounce, or 28 g)	7 g
Peanut butter (2 tablespoons, or 32 g)	8 g
Quinoa, cooked (3.5 ounces, or 100 g)	4 g
Seitan (3.5 ounces, or 100 g)	16 g
Soymilk, plain (1 cup, or 235 ml)	7 g
Split peas, cooked (1 cup, or 196 g)	16 g
Tempeh (4 ounces, or 115 g)	21 g
Tofu (½ cup, or 126 g)	10 g
Walnuts (1 ounce, or 28 g)	4 g
Wild rice, cooked (3.5 ounces, or 100 g)	4 g

Sources: USDA National Nutrient Database for Standard Reference Release 26, and manufacturers' Nutrition Facts labels.

base (such as in our Quit-the-Cluck Seitan, page 138), we use Better than Bouillon No Chicken Base. We find these in the soup aisle of the grocery store. We also love to make the All-Season Blend recipe found in Joanne Stepaniak's *The Ultimate Uncheese Cookbook* and use that for a broth powder (using just a third of the salt called for). If you can't find the aforementioned products and don't want to make your own broth powder, try using crumbled vegan bouillon cubes instead, substituting 1 cube per 1 teaspoon of paste or powder.

Dried mushrooms: Fresh mushrooms are great, but we also often use them in dried form, as they pack quite a flavor punch. You'll see them featured in a few of our recipes (like our Mushroom Bean Spread, page 62), and we never let their soaking liquid go to waste, instead putting it to great use in more recipes (like our Giardiniera Chili, page 30). Here's how to reconstitute dried mushrooms and extract their fabulous flavor in liquid form: Quickly rinse 0.88 ounces (25 g) of any kind of dried mushrooms and place them in a medium bowl. Add 1 cup (235 ml) of vegetable broth on top, pressing on the mushrooms to make sure they can all absorb the broth, and soak for 20 minutes. Gently squeeze the liquid out of the mushrooms, without discarding it. Follow the instructions in the recipes after that (for both the mushrooms and liquid).

Fire-roasted tomatoes: You will notice the use of these extra flavorful canned tomatoes in some of our dishes, but we've been made aware that they're not available everywhere. One of our tester friends, Liz Wyman, recommends using regular diced tomatoes and adding a few drops of liquid smoke to make up for the lack of fire-roastedness. It does the trick superbly.

Harissa: Harissa is made from a blend of different hot peppers and other spices. It is originally from North Africa and varies in heat content, which is why we always use it "to taste." It is available in both a paste and a powder. We prefer the paste for its fresher flavor. You can usually find it in the ethnic aisle of well-stocked grocery stores.

Neutral-flavored oils: We're partial to neutral-flavored oils because they don't introduce much flavor to a dish, so they are incredibly versatile. Choose from corn oil, grapeseed oil, light olive oil, peanut oil, safflower oil, and more. If possible and affordable, we buy organic oils.

Sambal oelek: Sambal oelek is a hot chili paste typically made from chile peppers, distilled vinegar, and salt. It can be found in the ethnic aisle of most grocery stores.

Sriracha: A hot chili sauce from Thailand, sriracha is traditionally used as a dipping sauce, like ketchup. We use it to add zing to some of our dishes. It can be found in most grocery stores.

Sucanat: Sucanat is a brand name that stands for **Su**gar **Ca**ne **Nat**ural. This granular sugar contains all of the sugarcane's molasses. We don't recommend using regular brown sugar in its place in most of our recipes, unless otherwise mentioned, as the results can vary greatly.

Tahini: Tahini is a sesame seed paste most commonly used as an ingredient in hummus. It makes an appearance in our Hummus Bisque (page 24), Seed and Nut Ice Cream (page 93), and more. It has become quite popular in recent years and can now be purchased in most grocery stores.

Tamari: Tamari is a Japanese-style soy sauce. We find it to have a deeper, richer flavor than regular soy sauce. We prefer using gluten-free reduced-sodium tamari, then adding salt as desired. If you cannot find tamari, use reduced-sodium soy sauce in its place.

Vegan milks: If you are cooking with protein in mind, and aren't allergic to soy or don't object to using it, soymilk is the top choice because it contains the most protein out of all plant-based milks. We also happen to be partial to unsweetened almond or almond/coconut milks. Just be sure to use unsweetened plain for savory applications and (unsweetened or not) plain or vanilla-flavored in sweet applications.

RECIPE ICONS

As you turn the pages of this book, you will come across recipes labeled as follows:

Quick and Easy: These are recipes that take less than 30 minutes to whip up, provided you have intermediate cooking and/or baking skills.

Soy-Free Potential: These are recipes that are free of any soy products, provided soymilk isn't used wherever vegan milk is called for.

Gluten-Free Potential: These are recipes that can be free of gluten, provided the ingredients that may contain gluten are double-checked for safe use, and that the gluten-free ingredients that could have been cross-contaminated during manufacturing are purchased as certified gluten-free. Please be vigilant: Thoroughly check labels and contact the manufacturer, if needed, to make sure the ingredients in question are safe to use as gluten-free.

You'll also find protein content listed for each recipe, based on serving size. Note that when a range of servings is listed ("8 to 10 servings," for example), the protein content is based on the larger number of servings (10, in this case) and therefore the smaller serving size.

2

BUZZWORTHY BEANS AND LEGUMES

Keep Your Fingers on this Magical Pulse

As one of the oldest cultivated plants (a "mere" 7,000 years ago in some areas of the world), we would be hard-pressed not to feel awed by the superpowers of lentils, peas, and the almighty bean. Loaded with dietary fiber and protein, as well as an endless list of other nutritional benefits, there seems to be nothing legumes can't do for our well-being.

Cassoulet, Hurray!

Although French in origin, and possibly the most elegant casserole you'll ever devour, this dish is actually very adaptable. Feel free to use only the seitan or the sausage, doubling the one you use. We like using a variety of white beans in this hearty dish.

¼ cup (60 ml) olive oil, divided

4 ounces (113 g) Quit-the-Cluck Seitan (page 138), chopped

½ of a Smoky Sausage (page 140), chopped

1½ cups (240 g) chopped onion

2 ounces (57 g) minced shiitake mushrooms

2 large carrots, peeled, sliced into ¼-inch (6 mm) rounds

2 stalks celery, chopped

1½ cups (355 ml) vegetable broth, divided

1 teaspoon liquid smoke

3 cans (each 15 ounces, or 425 g) white beans of choice, drained and rinsed

1 can (14.5 ounces, or 410 g) diced tomatoes, undrained

2 tablespoons (32 g) tomato paste

1 tablespoon (15 ml) tamari

1 tablespoon (18 g) no chicken bouillon paste, or 2 bouillon cubes, crumbled

2 tablespoons (8 g) minced fresh parsley

2 teaspoons dried thyme

½ teaspoon dried rosemary

Salt and pepper

2 cups (200 g) fresh bread crumbs

½ cup (40 g) panko crumbs

YIELD: 8 to 10 servings
PROTEIN CONTENT PER SERVING: 22 g

Preheat the oven to 375°F (190°C, or gas mark 5).

Heat 1 tablespoon (15 ml) of olive oil in a large skillet over medium heat.

Add the seitan and sausage. Cook for 4 to 6 minutes, stirring occasionally, until browned. Transfer to a plate and set aside.

Add the onion and a pinch of salt to the same skillet. Cook for 5 to 7 minutes until translucent. Transfer to the same plate. Add the shiitakes, carrots, and celery to the skillet and cook for 2 minutes. Add 1 tablespoon (15 ml) vegetable broth and the liquid smoke. Cook for 2 to 3 minutes, stirring, until the liquid is absorbed or evaporated.

Return the seitan and onions to the skillet and add the beans, tomatoes, tomato paste, tamari, bouillon, parsley, thyme, rosemary, and remaining broth. Cook for 3 to 4 minutes, stirring to combine. Season with salt and pepper to taste and transfer to a large casserole pan.

Toss together the fresh bread crumbs, panko crumbs, and the remaining 3 tablespoons (45 ml) olive oil in a small bowl. Spread evenly over the bean mixture. Bake for 30 to 35 minutes until the crumbs are browned.

Double-Garlic Bean and Vegetable Soup

▶ GLUTEN-FREE POTENTIAL ▶ SOY-FREE POTENTIAL

With both fresh and roasted garlic, this hearty bean and vegetable soup can only be made better if it's served with some crusty bread. Sit back and prepare to be wowed by this bean-centric bowl of Italian-influenced soup.

1 tablespoon (15 ml) olive oil

1 teaspoon fine sea salt

1½ cups (240 g) minced onion

5 cloves garlic, minced

2 cups (220 g) chopped russet potatoes

¾ cup (96 g) sliced carrots

½ cup (60 g) chopped celery

1 teaspoon Italian seasoning blend

½ teaspoon red pepper flakes, or to taste

⅛ teaspoon celery seed

4 cups water (940 ml), divided

1 can (14.5 ounces, or 410 g) crushed tomatoes or tomato purée

1 head roasted garlic (See Recipe Notes.)

2 tablespoons (30 g) prepared vegan pesto, plus more for garnish

2 cans (each 15 ounces, or 425 g) different kinds of white beans, drained and rinsed

½ cup (50 g) 1-inch (2.5 cm) pieces green beans

Salt and pepper

YIELD: 4 servings
PROTEIN CONTENT PER SERVING: 21 g

Heat the oil and salt in a large soup pot over medium heat. Add the onion, garlic, potatoes, carrots, and celery. Cook for 4 to 6 minutes, stirring occasionally, until the onions are translucent. Add the seasoning blend, red pepper flakes, and celery seed and stir for 2 minutes. Add 3 cups (705 ml) of the water and the crushed tomatoes.

Combine the remaining 1 cup (235 ml) water and the roasted garlic in a blender. Process until smooth. Add to the soup mixture and bring to a boil. Reduce the heat to simmer and cook for 30 minutes.

Stir in the pesto, beans, and green beans. Simmer for 15 minutes. Taste and adjust the seasonings. Serve each bowl with a dollop of pesto, if desired.

Recipe Notes

• In this recipe, it's best to use good quality pesto. Every year, Tami makes a big batch of pesto and freezes it in ice cube trays. Pop them out and freeze them in an airtight container for easy-to-use portions.

• To make roasted garlic: Preheat the oven to 400°F (200°C, or gas mark 6). Cut the top skin away from the head of garlic to reveal some of the cloves. Place the head on an 8-inch (20 cm) piece of foil. Drizzle with ½ teaspoon olive oil and season with salt and pepper. Fold closed. Bake for 30 minutes or until golden. It's handy to roast a couple heads of garlic and keep them in the refrigerator to add flavor to an array of dishes.

Hummus Bisque

▶ QUICK AND EASY   ▶ SOY-FREE POTENTIAL   ▶ GLUTEN-FREE POTENTIAL

This creamy, rich-tasting, but also surprisingly light bisque, can be made a bit greener and even more fiber-rich when served with broccoli. Use roasted or steamed chopped florets and add after blending, right before serving.

1 tablespoon (15 ml) toasted sesame oil

¼ cup (40 g) chopped shallot

2 teaspoons grated or pressed garlic

1 teaspoon ground cumin

1 teaspoon sambal oelek or harissa paste, or to taste

½ teaspoon smoked paprika

2 cups (328 g) cooked chickpeas

⅓ cup (80 ml) fresh lemon juice

3 cups (705 ml) vegetable broth, more if needed

½ cup (128 g) tahini

Salt and white pepper

¼ cup (4 g) chopped fresh cilantro or (15 g) parsley (or a combination of the two), for garnish

Toasted cumin seeds, for garnish, optional

Lemon zest, for garnish, optional

YIELD: 4 servings
PROTEIN CONTENT PER SERVING: 14 g

Heat the oil in a large pot. Add the shallot, garlic, cumin, sambal oelek or harissa paste, paprika, and chickpeas. Cook on medium heat, stirring often, until the shallot is tender and the preparation is fragrant, about 4 minutes. Add the lemon juice, stirring to combine.

Add the broth and bring to a boil. Lower the heat, cover with a lid, and simmer for 10 minutes. Add the tahini, stirring to combine. Note that the tahini might look curdled when you add it, but it will be okay after simmering and blending. Cover with the lid and simmer for another 5 minutes.

Use a handheld blender and blend the mixture until smooth. Be careful: The liquid will be hot, so watch for spatters! You can also use a regular blender to purée the soup, just be careful while transferring the hot liquid. If you find the bisque a little thick for your taste once blended, add extra broth as needed.

Adjust the seasonings to taste and serve garnished with cilantro, parsley, cumin seeds, and lemon zest.

Leftovers can be slowly reheated by simmering in a small saucepan for about 6 minutes until heated through. Stir occasionally while reheating and be careful not to scorch what is a rather thick soup.

Mean Bean Minestrone

We've packed this colorful, stew-like minestrone with cannellini beans and cooked farro for a healthy dose of protein and fiber. Sprinkling some of our Nut and Seed Sprinkles (page 82) on top further boosts the protein profile of this dish. Be sure to thoroughly wash the leek in a sieve once it's sliced in order to remove the grit that hides between its layers!

1 tablespoon (15 ml) olive oil

½ cup (80 g) chopped red onion

4 cloves garlic, grated or pressed

1 leek, white and light green parts, trimmed and chopped (about 4 ounces, or 113 g)

2 carrots, peeled and minced (about 4 ounces, or 113 g)

2 ribs of celery, minced (about 2 ounces, or 57 g)

2 yellow squashes, trimmed and chopped (about 8 ounces, or 227 g)

1 green bell pepper, trimmed and chopped (about 8 ounces, or 227 g)

1 tablespoon (16 g) tomato paste

1 teaspoon dried oregano

1 teaspoon dried basil

½ teaspoon smoked paprika

⅛ to ¼ teaspoon cayenne pepper, or to taste

2 cans (each 15 ounces, or 425 g) diced fire-roasted tomatoes

4 cups (940 ml) vegetable broth, more if needed

3 cups (532 g) cannellini beans, or other white beans

2 cups (330 g) cooked farro, or other whole grain or pasta

Salt, to taste

Nut and Seed Sprinkles (page 82), for garnish, optional and to taste

In a large pot, add the oil, onion, garlic, leek, carrots, celery, yellow squash, bell pepper, tomato paste, oregano, basil, paprika, and cayenne pepper. Cook on medium-high heat, stirring often, until the vegetables start to get tender, about 6 minutes.

Add the tomatoes and broth. Bring to a boil, lower the heat, cover with a lid, and simmer 15 minutes.

Add the beans and simmer another 10 minutes. Add the farro and simmer 5 more minutes to heat the farro.

Note that this is a thick minestrone. If there are leftovers (which taste even better, by the way), the soup will thicken more once chilled.

Add extra broth if you prefer a thinner soup, and adjust seasoning if needed. Add Nut and Seed Sprinkles on each portion upon serving, if desired.

Store leftovers in an airtight container in the refrigerator for up to 5 days. The minestrone can also be frozen for up to 3 months.

YIELD: 8 to 10 servings

PROTEIN CONTENT PER SERVING: 9 g

Sushi Rice and Bean Stew

▶ GLUTEN-FREE POTENTIAL

We've paired up our go-to sushi rice with a lovely vegetable stew that makes for great, protein-rich, comfort food. Enjoy it in your favorite large soup bowl, while curled up in a blanket. Think of it as an Asian-flavored, cruelty-free, noodleless version of chicken noodle soup. We're told it is reminiscent of hot and sour soup, too!

You can easily double the sushi rice recipe if you'd like more rice with each serving. And be sure not to miss the Recipe Note if you want to add the soaked mushrooms to the stew.

FOR THE SUSHI RICE:

1 cup (208 g) dry sushi rice, thoroughly rinsed until water runs clear and drained

1¼ cups (295 ml) water

1 tablespoon (15 ml) fresh lemon juice

1 teaspoon toasted sesame oil

1 teaspoon sriracha

1 teaspoon tamari

1 teaspoon agave nectar or brown rice syrup

To make the sushi rice: Combine the rice and water in a rice cooker, cover with the lid, and cook until the water is absorbed without lifting the lid. (Alternatively, cook the rice on the stove top, following the directions on the package.)

While the rice is cooking, combine the remaining sushi rice ingredients in a large bowl.

Let the rice steam for 10 minutes in the rice cooker with the lid still on. Gently fold the cooked rice into the dressing. Set aside.

FOR THE STEW:

1 tablespoon (15 ml) toasted sesame oil

9 ounces (255 g) minced carrot (about 4 medium carrots)

½ cup (80 g) chopped red onion or ¼ cup (40 g) minced shallot

2 teaspoons grated fresh ginger or ¾ teaspoon ginger powder

4 cloves garlic, grated or pressed

1½ cups (246 g) cooked chickpeas

1 cup (155 g) frozen, shelled edamame

3 tablespoons (45 ml) seasoned rice vinegar

2 tablespoons (30 ml) tamari

2 teaspoons sriracha, or to taste

1 cup (235 ml) mushroom-soaking broth (See Recipe Note.)

2 cups (470 ml) vegetable broth

2 tablespoons (36 g) white miso

2 tablespoons (16 g) toasted white sesame seeds

YIELD: 4 to 6 servings

PROTEIN CONTENT PER SERVING: 11 g

To make the stew: Heat the oil in a large pot on medium-high heat. Add the carrots, onion, ginger, and garlic. Lower the heat to medium and cook until the vegetables just start to get tender, stirring often, about 4 minutes.

Add the chickpeas, edamame, vinegar, tamari, and sriracha. Stir and cook for another 4 minutes. Add the broths, and bring back to a slow boil. Cover with a lid, lower the heat, and simmer for 10 minutes.

Place the miso in a small bowl and remove 3 tablespoons (45 ml) of the broth from the pot. Stir into the miso to thoroughly combine. Stir the miso mixture back into the pot, and remove from the heat.

Divide the rice among 4 to 6 bowls, depending on your appetite. Add approximately 1 cup (235 ml) of the stew on top of each portion of rice. Add 1 teaspoon of sesame seeds on top of each serving, and serve immediately.

If you do not plan on eating this dish in one shot, keep the rice and stew separated and store in the refrigerator for up to 4 days.

When reheating the stew, do not bring to a boil. Slowly reheat the rice with the stew on medium heat in a small saucepan until heated through.

Recipe Note

To make the mushroom-soaking broth: Quickly rinse 0.88 ounce (25 g) dried shiitake mushrooms, and place them in a medium bowl. Add 1 cup (235 ml) of warm vegetable broth on top and soak for 15 minutes. Gently squeeze the broth out of the mushrooms, but do not discard the liquid. Set it aside. Chop the mushrooms and add them to the stew at the same time you add the broth, if desired.

Giardiniera Chili

▶ SOY-FREE POTENTIAL ▶ GLUTEN-FREE POTENTIAL

Giardiniera means "lady gardener" in Italian, and we felt it was an appropriate name for this vegetable-rich, mouthwatering chili. Not only does the mix of beans contribute to raising the protein content of this comfort food, but the nutritional yeast also helps with its 8 g of protein per 2 tablespoons (15 g). This chili is great to enjoy scooped on cooked rice, a whole grain, baked potatoes, or with cornbread.

1 tablespoon (15 ml) neutral-flavored oil

1 medium red onion, chopped

4 carrots, peeled and minced (9 ounces, or 250 g)

2 zucchini, trimmed and minced (11 ounces, or 320 g)

4 Roma tomatoes, diced (14 ounces, or 400 g)

4 cloves garlic, grated or pressed

1 tablespoon (8 g) mild to medium chili powder

1 teaspoon ground cumin

½ teaspoon smoked paprika

½ teaspoon liquid smoke

¼ teaspoon fine sea salt, or to taste

¼ teaspoon cayenne pepper, or to taste

2 tablespoons (32 g) tomato paste

1 can (15 ounces, or 425 g) diced fire-roasted tomatoes (see page 10)

½ cup (120 ml) vegetable broth

½ cup (120 ml) mushroom-soaking broth (see page 29) or extra vegetable broth

1 can (15 ounces, or 425 g) pinto beans, drained and rinsed

1 can (15 ounces, or 425 g) black beans, drained and rinsed

½ cup (60 g) nutritional yeast

YIELD: 8 servings

PROTEIN CONTENT PER SERVING: 28 g

Heat the oil on medium-high in a large pot and add the onion, carrots, zucchini, tomatoes, and garlic. Cook for 6 minutes, stirring occasionally, until the carrots just start to get tender. Add the chili powder, cumin, paprika, liquid smoke, salt, cayenne pepper, and tomato paste, stirring to combine. Cook another 2 minutes. Add the diced tomatoes, broths, beans, and nutritional yeast. Bring to a low boil. Lower the heat, cover with a lid, and simmer 15 minutes, stirring occasionally. Remove the lid and simmer for another 5 minutes.

Serve on top of cooked whole grain of choice or with your favorite chili accompaniments.

Leftovers can be stored in an airtight container in the refrigerator for up to 4 days or frozen for up to 3 months.

Shorba (Lentil Soup)

▶ SOY-FREE POTENTIAL ▶ GLUTEN-FREE POTENTIAL

The earthy flavor of humble lentils shines through in this recipe. We've added simple vegetables and the all-important spice blend of Ethiopia, berbere, to give this dish an amazing depth of flavor that will keep you coming back for more.

1 tablespoon (15 ml) olive oil

1 medium onion, minced

1 large carrot, peeled and chopped

1 fist-size russet potato, cut into small cubes (about 7 ounces, or 198 g)

4 large cloves garlic, minced

2 teaspoons grated fresh ginger root

1 to 2 teaspoons berbere, to taste (See Recipe Notes.)

½ teaspoon turmeric

1 cup (192 g) brown lentils, picked over and rinsed (See Recipe Notes.)

6 cups (1.4 L) water, more if desired

1 tablespoon (16 g) tomato paste

1 tablespoon (18 g) vegetable bouillon paste, or 2 bouillon cubes

Salt and pepper

YIELD: 4 to 6 servings

PROTEIN CONTENT PER SERVING: 10 g

Heat the oil in a large soup pot over medium heat. Add the onion, carrot, and potato. Cook for 5 to 7 minutes, stirring occasionally, until the onions are translucent. Stir in the garlic, ginger, berbere, turmeric, and lentils and cook and stir for 1 minute until fragrant. Add the water, tomato paste, and bouillon. Bring to a boil, and then reduce the heat to a simmer. Cook for 30 minutes, stirring occasionally, until the lentils are tender. Taste and adjust the seasonings.

Recipe Notes

• Berbere is a complex and very flavorful spice blend from Ethiopia. The heat level of berbere varies, so it is always important to use it to your own taste. It can be found in the ethnic section of grocery stores and specialty shops. There are also many recipes online for making your own.

• For a thicker, stew-like dish, add 1 extra cup (192 g) lentils. Simmer the soup for 1 hour and mash some of the beans against the side of the pot.

Split Pea Patties

We love to serve these tester-favorite patties with Cashew Raita (page 91) or Simple Cashew Dip (page 124).

¾ cup (148 g) dry green split peas, cooked al dente (See Recipe Note.), drained

3 tablespoons (45 ml) fresh lemon juice

1 tablespoon (15 ml) neutral-flavored oil

3 cloves garlic, grated or pressed

⅓ cup (53 g) minced red onion

¼ cup (4 g) minced fresh cilantro or (15 g) fresh parsley

1 teaspoon ground cumin

1 teaspoon garam masala

½ teaspoon fine sea salt

½ teaspoon paprika (smoked or regular)

½ teaspoon turmeric

⅛ teaspoon cayenne pepper

¼ cup (30 g) whole wheat pastry flour or (31 g) all-purpose flour

2 tablespoons (24 g) potato starch or (16 g) cornstarch

½ teaspoon baking powder

Water, as needed

Nonstick cooking spray or oil spray

YIELD: 8 patties

PROTEIN CONTENT PER PATTY: 10 g

Place the cooked split peas in a food processor and pulse about 15 times to break down the peas slightly. You're not looking to purée them, but to make it so the mixture will hold together better to form patties. In a large bowl, combine the split peas with the lemon juice, oil, garlic, onion, cilantro, cumin, garam masala, salt, paprika, turmeric, and cayenne pepper until thoroughly mixed. Add the flour, starch, and baking powder on top.

Stir until thoroughly mixed. If the mixture is dry and crumbly, stir water into it, 1 tablespoon (15 ml) at a time until the mixture holds together better. We usually have to add 2 tablespoons (30 ml) of water. Refrigerate for 1 hour.

Preheat the oven to 350°F (180°C, or gas mark 4).

Divide the mixture into 8 patties (each one a scant but packed ¼ cup, or 60 g) of a little under 3 inches (7 cm) in diameter and ½-inch (1.3 cm) in thickness. Place on a baking sheet lined with parchment paper or press into a lightly greased whoopie pie pan. Lightly coat the top with cooking spray.

Bake for 15 minutes on one side, flip, lightly coat with cooking spray, and bake for another 10 minutes until golden brown.

Store leftovers in an airtight container in the refrigerator for up to 4 days. Gently reheat in a pan or in the oven or enjoy cold or at room temperature.

Recipe Note

It's important to only cook the split peas to al dente consistency here. Depending on freshness, this should take about 30 minutes. Place the rinsed and picked peas in a large saucepan, and cover fully with an extra inch (2.5 cm) of vegetable broth. Bring to a boil, cover with a lid, and simmer until al dente. Carefully spoon out a pea, let it cool a moment, and break it with your nail: It should break in two easily and in one clean break, without being mushy.

Savory Edamame Mini Cakes

▶ QUICK AND EASY

Edamame are immature, fresh soybeans. We love them not just for the protein punch, but for their fantastic flavor which is similar to greener, brighter-flavored lima beans. Here we've transformed them into crunchy, fritterlike cakes and added a dipping sauce to create a snack that will power you throughout the day.

FOR THE SAUCE:

3 tablespoons (45 ml) tamari

1 teaspoon smooth peanut butter

1 teaspoon seasoned rice vinegar, or to taste

1 teaspoon sambal oelek, or to taste

FOR THE CAKES:

1 cup (150 g) frozen, shelled edamame, thawed

¼ cup (36 g) minced bell pepper (any color)

3 tablespoons (30 g) minced red onion

2 cloves garlic, minced

½ teaspoon 5-spice powder

Generous ¼ teaspoon fine sea salt

Pinch of ground black pepper

1 cup (140 g) whole spelt flour

⅓ cup plus 1 tablespoon (95 ml) unsweetened plain vegan milk

⅔ cup (53 g) panko crumbs

2 tablespoons (16 g) toasted sesame seeds

2 tablespoons (30 ml) high-heat neutral-flavored oil

YIELD: 14 to 16 cakes, plus ¼ cup (60 ml) sauce

PROTEIN CONTENT PER CAKE (WITH SAUCE): 3 g

To make the sauce: In a small bowl, whisk together the tamari, peanut butter, rice vinegar, and sambal oelek until smooth. Set aside.

To make the cakes: Put the edamame, bell pepper, onion, garlic, 5-spice powder, salt, and pepper in a medium-size bowl. Stir to combine. Stir in the flour, then the milk to form a dough. It should be shape-able, but some of the edamame may poke out. Combine the panko and the sesame seeds on a shallow plate.

Heat the oil in a large skillet over medium-high heat.

Scoop 1 tablespoon (26 g) of the mixture and shape it into a small round no more than ½ inch (1.3 cm) thick and about 1½ inches (3.8 cm) in diameter. Put it in the panko mixture and pat to coat well on both sides, continuing to shape it into a small cake. Repeat until all the cakes have been formed. Put half of the cakes into the skillet and cook for 3 to 5 minutes until golden brown. Turn over to cook the second side for 2 to 4 minutes, until also golden brown. Drain on a paper towel–lined plate. Cook the remaining cakes in the same manner, adding more oil if needed. Serve with the sauce for dipping.

Recipe Notes

• These will seem fragile when you are shaping them, but they end up quite firm.

• You can decrease the panko and the sesame seed mixture, as this will be more than you will need, but don't reduce it dramatically or you will run out. If the mixture is soggy, discard it. If not, it can be stored in an airtight container and used in breading other dishes.

Quinoa Edamame Rolls

▶ GLUTEN-FREE POTENTIAL

Panfried-to-a-crisp spring rolls are one of our favorite comfort foods, and this new combination joins the ranks of the ones we love the most. You'll find that edamame, nutty quinoa, and crunchy toasted almonds pair up extremely well, not only on a protein and flavor level, but also on the textural front.

FOR THE DRESSING:

4½ tablespoons (68 ml) fresh lemon juice

1½ tablespoons (23 ml) toasted sesame oil

1½ tablespoons (23 ml) sriracha

1½ tablespoons (23 ml) tamari

1½ tablespoons (30 g) agave nectar or brown rice syrup

1½ tablespoons (12 g) toasted sesame seeds

1 large clove garlic, grated or pressed

FOR THE ROLLS:

¾ cup (116 g) cooked shelled edamame

¾ cup (110 g) packed cooked and cooled quinoa

½ cup (45 g) packed minced napa cabbage

¼ cup (27 g) toasted slivered almonds

¼ cup (20 g) chopped scallion

2 tablespoons (2 g) loosely packed chopped cilantro

2 tablespoons (24 g) packed peeled and grated daikon radish, liquid gently squeezed out before measuring

14 spring roll wrappers

Nonstick cooking spray or oil spray

YIELD: 14 rolls, plus scant ¾ cup (175 ml) dressing

PROTEIN CONTENT PER ROLL (WITH DRESSING): 4 g

To make the dressing: Combine all the ingredients in a small bowl, using a whisk. Set aside.

To make the rolls: Combine the edamame, quinoa, napa cabbage, almonds, scallion, cilantro, and daikon radish in a large bowl. Add ¼ cup (60 ml) of the dressing on top, stirring to combine. Set aside the rest of the dressing for serving.

Immerse the spring roll wrappers 1 sheet at a time in warm water to soften. Soak for a few seconds, until pliable. Handle carefully because the wraps tear easily. Drain on a clean kitchen towel before rolling.

To assemble, place 2 packed tablespoons (30 g) of filling per moistened wrapper.

Roll tightly and place on a plate. Repeat with remaining rolls. Be careful when separating the rolls: The wraps might stick to one another a little, but won't tear if you separate them slowly.

Heat a large skillet on medium-high heat. Lower the heat to medium, lightly coat with cooking spray or oil spray, away from the heat. Place as many rolls as will fit in your skillet without overcrowding it, and cook the rolls on each side until light golden brown and crisp, about 4 minutes per side. Repeat with remaining rolls. Serve immediately with the remaining dressing.

Leftovers can be wrapped tightly and stored in the refrigerator for up to 3 days.

Spicy Chickpea Fries

▶ GLUTEN-FREE POTENTIAL

The cool thing about these crispy bean-based fries (on top of their perfect amount of spice) is that you don't have to bake them all at once. Just cut and bake as needed. The leftovers will keep well for up to 1 week, stored in an airtight container in the refrigerator. Serve them with our Cashew Raita (page 91) for dipping!

4 cups (940 ml) vegetable broth

2 tablespoons (15 g) nutritional yeast

1 teaspoon fine sea salt

1 teaspoon onion powder

1 teaspoon garlic powder

1 teaspoon smoked paprika

1 teaspoon ground cumin

1 teaspoon ground coriander

1 teaspoon garam masala

2 cups (240 g) chickpea flour, sifted

¼ cup (30 g) corn flour, sifted
(not cornstarch, preferably organic)

Nonstick cooking spray

Up to ¼ cup (60 ml) olive oil,
for brushing

YIELD: About 64 fries, or 4 servings
PROTEIN CONTENT PER SERVING: 14 g

Combine the broth, nutritional yeast, salt, onion powder, garlic powder, paprika, cumin, coriander, and garam masala in a large saucepan and bring to a boil. Lower the heat, and then (and this is important to avoid clumping) *slowly* stream in the flours, whisking constantly. Reduce the heat to medium-low, switch to stirring with a wooden spoon almost constantly, and cook for 6 minutes or until the mixture is so thick that when you slash a line through its center with the spoon all the way to the bottom of the pan, the line remains and the mixture doesn't slide back to cover the bottom of the pan. Be sure to adjust the temperature, if needed, to avoid scorching.

Remove from the heat. Spread evenly in an 8-inch (20 cm) square baking pan coated with cooking spray, using an angled spatula. Do not cover the pan. Once it's cool enough, place it in the refrigerator for at least 2 hours.

Remove the chilled mixture from the pan. Cut into ½-inch (1.3 cm) strips, flipping those strips on the side (they will be approximately 1-inch [2.5 cm] wide once flipped) and cutting them in two lengthwise again to obtain two ½-inch (1.3 cm) wide, 8-inch (20 cm) long strips. Then cut both strips once in the middle widthwise. You should get fries of approximately 4 × ½ inches (10 × 1.3 cm).

Preheat the oven to 425°F (220°C, or gas mark 7). Lightly grease a large rimmed baking sheet with olive oil.

Lightly brush the fries with oil and space them evenly on the prepared sheet.

Bake for 15 minutes, flip the fries, and bake for another 15 minutes or until golden brown and crispy. Serve immediately.

Baked Falafel

▶ QUICK AND EASY

These falafel are bursting with fresh flavors, loaded with fiber, and packed with protein. We chose to bake them rather than fry them, and they're not missing anything as far as awesomeness goes. Enjoy them dipped in Cashew Raita (page 91) or Simple Cashew Dip (page 124).

Nonstick cooking spray

3 cups (492 g) cooked chickpeas

¼ cup (60 ml) fresh lemon juice

3 cloves garlic, minced

⅓ cup (20 g) packed fresh parsley

⅓ cup (5 g) packed fresh cilantro

⅓ cup (53 g) minced red onion

2 tablespoons (32 g) tahini

1 tablespoon (15 ml) toasted sesame oil

1½ teaspoons ground cumin

1½ teaspoons ground coriander

¼ teaspoon cayenne pepper

Scant ½ teaspoon fine sea salt, or to taste

3 tablespoons (23 g) whole wheat pastry flour or all-purpose flour

½ teaspoon baking soda

2 tablespoons (30 ml) olive oil

YIELD: 32 falafels

PROTEIN CONTENT PER FALAFEL: 2 g

Preheat the oven to 400°F (200°C, or gas mark 6). Lightly coat 32 cups out of two 24-cup mini muffin tins with cooking spray.

Place the chickpeas, lemon juice, garlic, parsley, and cilantro in a food processor.

Consider doing this in a couple of batches, depending on the size of your food processor. Pulse a few times, stopping to scrape the sides with a rubber spatula: You're looking for a somewhat smooth texture but not exactly a paste. The beans should be broken down, but it's fine if a few pieces remain as long as the mixture is cohesive.

Remove from the food processor and place in a large bowl. Add the onion, tahini, sesame oil, cumin, coriander, cayenne pepper, and salt. Stir to combine. Add the flour and baking soda on top and stir until thoroughly combined.

Gather 1 packed tablespoon (18 g) of mixture per falafel, gently shape into a ball and place in the mini muffin tin. Repeat with remaining mixture. Lightly brush the tops with olive oil.

Bake for 15 minutes, carefully flip each falafel, and lightly brush with oil. Bake for another 8 minutes or until golden brown.

Remove from the oven and let stand 5 minutes before serving.

Pudla

▶ QUICK AND EASY ▶ GLUTEN-FREE POTENTIAL

Pudla is a super tasty Indian cross between a fluffy omelet and a savory pancake. We've packed our version with colorful spices and big bursts of flavor. We love to serve it with Eggplant Balela (page 59), Cashew Raita (page 91), or Simple Cashew Dip (page 124).

¾ cup (180 ml) unsweetened plain vegan milk, plus extra if needed

2 tablespoons (30 ml) fresh lemon juice

1 cup (120 g) chickpea flour

½ teaspoon baking soda

½ teaspoon ground cumin

½ teaspoon ground coriander

½ teaspoon garam masala

⅛ to ¼ teaspoon cayenne pepper, or to taste

½ teaspoon fine sea salt, or to taste

2 tablespoons (30 ml) olive oil

2 tablespoons (15 g) nutritional yeast

1 tablespoon (16 g) tahini

¼ cup (40 g) minced red onion

¼ cup (4 g) fresh cilantro leaves (not packed)

2 cloves garlic, grated or pressed

Nonstick cooking spray or oil spray

YIELD: 2 to 4 servings
PROTEIN CONTENT PER SERVING: 9 g

Combine the milk and lemon juice in a medium bowl. Let stand for two minutes to let the milk curdle. This is your "buttermilk."

In the meantime, whisk together the flour, baking soda, cumin, coriander, garam masala, cayenne pepper, and salt in a large bowl.

Add the olive oil, nutritional yeast, tahini, red onion, cilantro, and garlic to the buttermilk.

Stir the wet ingredients into the dry until well combined, but do not overmix. Let stand 10 minutes. The batter will be thick. If it is so thick it becomes unmanageable, add extra milk as needed to thin out, up to ¼ cup (60 ml).

Heat a large nonstick pan on medium-high heat. Lower the heat to medium. Lightly coat the pan with cooking spray or oil spray once hot, away from the heat. Add ¼ of the batter (about 3.5 ounces, or 100 g), spreading it into a circle of slightly over 5 inches (13 cm). Let cook for approximately 4 minutes until the center bubbles and looks not too dry but not too moist either. Carefully lift the edges of the pudla to make sure it is light golden brown, which is another sign it is ready to flip.

Carefully flip with a spatula and let cook for another 4 minutes or until golden brown on that side too.

Lightly coat the pan again each time before cooking the rest of the batter in three batches. Serve immediately.

The Whole Enchilada

Granted, this recipe has a few steps that make it more of a weekend endeavor, but it is an extremely worthy and rewarding one at that. We loved every single layer of these enchiladas, from the "beantastic" filling to the delectable red sauce. We were especially taken with the creamy, rich, cashew-based sauce that serves as a topping—reminding us of a slightly spicier cousin to the charmer that is Italian lasagna.

FOR THE SAUCE:

2 tablespoons (30 ml) olive oil

½ cup (80 g) chopped red onion

4 ounces (113 g) tomato paste

1 tablespoon (15 ml) adobo sauce

1 tablespoon (8 g) mild to medium chili powder

1 teaspoon ground cumin

3 cloves garlic, grated or pressed

½ teaspoon fine sea salt, or to taste

2 tablespoons (15 g) whole wheat pastry flour or (16 g) all-purpose flour

2 cups (470 ml) water

To make the sauce: Heat the oil on medium heat in a large skillet. Add the onion and cook until fragrant while stirring occasionally, about 2 minutes. Add the tomato paste, adobo sauce, chili powder, cumin, garlic, and salt. Sauté for 2 minutes, stirring frequently. Sprinkle the flour on top and cook 2 minutes, stirring frequently. Slowly whisk in the water and cook until slightly thickened, about 6 minutes, whisking frequently to prevent clumps. Remove from the heat and set aside.

FOR THE FILLING:

1½ teaspoons olive oil

⅓ cup (53 g) chopped red onion

1 sweet potato, trimmed and peeled, chopped (about 8.8 ounces, or 250 g)

1 yellow squash, trimmed and chopped (about 5.3 ounces, or 150 g)

2 cloves garlic, grated or pressed

1 tablespoon (8 g) nutritional yeast

½ teaspoon smoked paprika

¼ teaspoon liquid smoke

Pinch of fine sea salt, or to taste

1½ cups (258 g) cooked black beans

3 tablespoons (45 ml) enchilada sauce (the one you just made)

12 to 14 corn tortillas (See Recipe Note.)

1 recipe Creamy Cashew Sauce (page 92)

Chopped fresh cilantro, to taste

Hot sauce, to taste

YIELD: 12 to 14 enchiladas

PROTEIN CONTENT PER ENCHILADA: 6 g

To make the filling: Heat the oil in a large skillet on medium heat. Add the onion and sweet potato and cook 6 minutes or until the potato just starts to get tender, stirring occasionally. Add the squash and garlic and cook for 4 minutes, stirring occasionally. Add the nutritional yeast, paprika, liquid smoke, and salt, stir to combine, and cook for another minute. Add the beans and enchilada sauce and stir to combine. Cover the pan, and simmer until the vegetables are completely tender, about 4 minutes. Add a little water if the vegetables stick to the skillet. Adjust the seasonings if needed.

Preheat the oven to 350°F (180°C, or gas mark 4).

Place the sauce in a large shallow bowl. If you aren't using pre-shaped, uncooked tortillas, follow the instructions in the Recipe Note to soften the tortillas so that they are easier to work with. Ladle about ⅓ cup (80 ml) of enchilada sauce on the bottom of a 9 × 13-inch (23 × 33 cm) baking dish. Dip each tortilla in the sauce to coat only lightly. Don't be too generous and gently scrape off the excess sauce with a spatula; otherwise, you will run out of sauce. Add a scant ¼ cup (about 45 g) of the filling in each tortilla. Fold the tortilla over the filling, rolling like a cigar. Place the enchiladas in the pan, seam side down. Make sure to squeeze them in tight so that there's room in the dish for all of them. Top evenly with the remaining enchilada sauce. Add the Creamy Cashew Sauce evenly on top.

Bake for 20 to 25 minutes or until the top is set and the enchiladas are heated through. Garnish with cilantro and serve with hot sauce.

Recipe Note

If you can find preshaped, uncooked corn tortillas that you need to quickly pan-fry before use, we strongly recommend them. Be sure to follow the instructions on the package. These tortillas are far sturdier and fresher-tasting and won't have a tendency to crack like the store-bought, ready-to-eat tortillas often do. If all you can find is the latter, be sure to warm them up in a heated pan (on medium heat, about 30 seconds on each side) to soften them up a bit before use.

Mujaddara

▶ SOY-FREE POTENTIAL ▶ GLUTEN-FREE POTENTIAL

This popular and seasoned-to-perfection Middle Eastern lentil-rice dish is great served with Eggplant Balela (page 59), or with the marinated eggplant alone (from the same recipe), combined with some of our Creamy Cashew Sauce (page 92), to taste. As an alternative to garnishing with nuts, you can also serve it with Cashew Raita (page 91) or Simple Cashew Dip (page 124). Not to brag, but we were told by someone who ate the most authentic Mujaddara straight from the source that ours was even better. (Actually, we're totally bragging.)

¾ cup (144 g) dry green lentils, rinsed and picked through

¾ cup (150 g) dry brown jasmine rice, rinsed and picked through

3 cups (705 ml) vegetable broth

1 tablespoon (15 ml) olive oil or melted coconut oil

2 white onions, chopped (10 ounces, or 340 g)

1 leek, thoroughly cleaned and sliced thinly, white and light green parts (6 ounces, or 170 g)

Vegetable broth or water, as needed

4 cloves garlic, grated or pressed

½ teaspoon fine sea salt, or to taste

½ teaspoon ground cinnamon

½ teaspoon ground cumin

½ teaspoon ground coriander

½ teaspoon paprika

¼ teaspoon cayenne pepper, or to taste

2 tablespoons (12 g) chopped fresh mint

2 tablespoons (8 g) chopped fresh parsley or (2 g) cilantro

Zest and juice of a small organic lemon

¼ cup (35 g) chopped toasted peanuts, cashews, or pine nuts, optional

YIELD: 4 to 6 servings
PROTEIN CONTENT PER SERVING: 11 g

Place the lentils and rice in a rice cooker. Cover with the broth, and stir to combine. Cover with the lid and cook until tender, 40 to 45 minutes. (Alternatively, cook the lentils and rice on the stove top, following the directions on the package of rice.)

In a large skillet, add the oil and heat on medium heat. Add the onions and leek and sauté until browned, about 15 minutes. Add vegetable broth, 1 tablespoon (15 ml) at a time, as needed, if the onions stick to the pan during that time. Add the garlic, salt, cinnamon, cumin, coriander, paprika, and cayenne pepper, stirring to combine. Stop stirring and cook until the onions are crisped and the spices toasted and fragrant, about 5 minutes.

Place the lentils and rice in a large bowl and add the spiced onions on top; thoroughly and gently fold the onions into the lentils and rice. Once you are ready to serve, fold the mint, parsley or cilantro, zest, and lemon juice into the mujaddara, and garnish each serving with nuts. Adjust the seasonings as needed.

Leftovers can be stored in an airtight container in the refrigerator for up to 4 days. Note that this dish tastes even better when it gets to sit for a while. Gently reheat before serving.

Black Bean and Avocado Salad

▶ QUICK AND EASY ▶ SOY-FREE POTENTIAL ▶ GLUTEN-FREE POTENTIAL

This is like guacamole, but it's not. It's also like black bean salsa, but it's not. It's the best of both in salad form.

1 cup (172 g) cooked black beans

½ cup (82 g) frozen corn (run under hot water, drained)

3 tablespoons (15 g) minced scallion

6 cherry tomatoes, cut into quarters

2 cloves garlic, minced

1 teaspoon minced fresh cilantro, or to taste

Pinch of dried oregano

1 chipotle in adobo

1 tablespoon (15 ml) fresh lemon juice

1 tablespoon (15 ml) apple cider vinegar

1 tablespoon (15 ml) vegetable broth

1 teaspoon nutritional yeast

2 tablespoons (15 g) roasted salted pepitas (hulled pumpkin seeds)

2 avocados, pitted, peeled, and chopped

Salt and pepper

YIELD: 4 servings

PROTEIN CONTENT PER SERVING: 8 g

Combine the beans, corn, scallion, cherry tomatoes, garlic, cilantro, and oregano in a medium-size bowl. Using a small blender or a mortar and pestle, thoroughly combine the chipotle, lemon juice, vinegar, broth, and nutritional yeast to form a dressing. Pour over the bean mixture and stir in the pepitas. Gently stir in the avocados. Season to taste with salt and pepper. Serve promptly so that the avocado doesn't discolor.

Recipe Note

If desired, crush a handful of tortilla chips over each serving for an added crunch.

Mediterranean Quinoa and Bean Salad

▶ SOY-FREE POTENTIAL ▶ GLUTEN-FREE POTENTIAL

If you're longing for something that will last for days in the refrigerator and be at the ready when you're hungry, look no further than this filling, yet light salad!

1¼ cups (213 g) dry ivory quinoa, rinsed

2½ cups (590 ml) vegetable broth

2 tablespoons (30 ml) apple cider vinegar

2 tablespoons (30 ml) fresh lemon juice

3 tablespoons (45 ml) extra-virgin olive oil

¼ cup (40 g) finely chopped red onion

2 to 3 cloves garlic, minced, or to taste

½ teaspoon red pepper flakes, or to taste

Salt and pepper

1½ cups (266 g) cooked cannellini beans

24 jumbo pitted kalamata olives, minced

Half of a red bell pepper, cored and diced

Half of a yellow bell pepper, cored and diced

8 ounces (227 g) mini heirloom tomatoes, halved or quartered depending on size

6 tablespoons (24 g) minced fresh parsley

15 leaves fresh basil, cut in chiffonade

YIELD: 6 to 8 servings
PROTEIN CONTENT PER SERVING: 6 g

Combine the quinoa with the broth in a medium saucepan. Bring to a boil and then reduce the heat to a simmer. Cover and cook until all liquid is absorbed, 12 to 15 minutes. The quinoa should be tender and translucent, and the germ ring should be visible along the outside edge of the grain. Set aside to cool completely.

In a large bowl, combine the vinegar, lemon juice, oil, onion, garlic, red pepper flakes, salt, and pepper. Stir the beans into the dressing. Add the cooled quinoa, olives, bell peppers, tomatoes, and parsley into the bowl with the beans. Fold with a rubber spatula to thoroughly yet gently combine.

Cover and chill for an hour to let the flavors meld. Garnish with basil upon serving. Leftovers can be stored in an airtight container in the refrigerator for up to 4 days.

Recipe Notes

• If you cannot find mini heirloom tomatoes, use the same weight of regular mini tomatoes or even standard-size chopped tomatoes of choice. You can remove the seeds if you prefer. (We just hate wasting anything, that's why we rarely bother.)

• For this salad, it's best to make the quinoa ahead of time and allow it to cool in an airtight container overnight. Cooled quinoa is less likely to absorb too much of the dressing, which would make for a salad that's a little dry.

• To boost the flavor of the beans, you can also combine the dressing and the beans the night before. Just be sure to cover the bowl and store it in the refrigerator.

Tabbouleh Verde

▶ QUICK AND EASY ▶ SOY-FREE POTENTIAL

It's actually kind of easy being green. Although, this tabbouleh isn't technically entirely *verde*: We've used black beans because we love their inimitable flavor and texture! If you're having a hard time locating heirloom green tomatoes, or you aren't a fan of the particular taste of green bell pepper, you can replace those with something else. In which case, you'll need to change the name of the tabbouleh before serving it, or it might be a little confusing for those who partake . . . .

1 cup (186 g) dry whole wheat couscous

½ cup (120 ml) vegetable broth, brought to a boil

3 tablespoons (45 ml) extra-virgin olive oil

2 tablespoons (30 ml) fresh lemon juice

2 tablespoons (30 ml) fresh lime juice

1½ cups (258 g) cooked black beans

1¼ cups (225 g) diced heirloom green tomato (Any other color will do.)

1 cup (150 g) diced green bell pepper (Any other color will do.)

⅓ cup (5 g) loosely packed fresh cilantro leaves, minced

¼ cup (20 g) minced scallion

1 small jalapeño, seeded and minced

½ teaspoon toasted cumin seeds

Salt and pepper, optional

Roasted pepitas (hulled pumpkin seeds), for garnish

1 lemon, cut into 4 to 6 wedges

1 lime, cut into 4 to 6 wedges

YIELD: 4 to 6 servings

PROTEIN CONTENT PER SERVING: 9 g

Mix the couscous with the broth in a large glass bowl. Add the oil, lemon juice, and lime juice. Stir well. Cover and let stand 5 minutes until the liquids are absorbed. Fluff with a fork.

Add the beans, tomato, bell pepper, cilantro, scallion, and jalapeño on top. Rub the cumin seeds between your fingers while adding them to release the flavor. Fold to combine with a rubber spatula. Adjust the seasonings to taste. Refrigerate for at least 30 minutes to chill and to let the flavors meld.

Serve and garnish each portion with a small handful of pepitas and a wedge of lemon and lime to drizzle before eating.

Leftovers can be stored in an airtight container in the refrigerator for up to 4 days.

Recipe Note

If you don't like cilantro, replace it with the same amount of fresh curly or Italian parsley.

Curried Bean and Corn Salad

▶ SOY-FREE POTENTIAL

Freekeh is an ancient grain from the Middle East. The young wheat has a slightly smoky, nutty taste. It holds its shape well, making it an ideal grain for salads. Here we combine it with crisp fresh vegetables, delicate sweet corn, and a blend of Indian spices to create a delectable dish.

½ cup (90 g) whole freekeh
(See Recipe Notes.)

3 cups (705 ml) salted water

1 can (15 ounce, or 425 g) chickpeas, drained and rinsed

1 cup (164 g) fresh or frozen corn (run under hot water, drained)

¼ cup (40 g) minced red onion

¼ cup (32 g) minced celery

¼ cup (38 g) minced bell pepper (any color)

3 tablespoons (12 g) minced fresh parsley

1 tablespoon (6 g) curry powder (mild or hot)

1 teaspoon ground cumin

1 teaspoon garam masala

½ teaspoon ginger powder

½ teaspoon fine sea salt

1 clove garlic

2 tablespoons (30 ml) seasoned rice vinegar

3 tablespoons (45 ml) olive oil

YIELD: 4 servings

PROTEIN CONTENT PER SERVING: 27 g

Bring the freekeh and salted water to a boil in a medium-size saucepan. Reduce to simmer and cook for 45 minutes, stirring occasionally, until tender. Drain and run under cold water, draining again. Transfer to a medium-size bowl. Add the chickpeas, corn, onion, celery, bell pepper, and parsley.

Heat the curry powder, cumin, and garam masala in a small skillet over medium heat. Stir and cook for 3 to 4 minutes until fragrant. Do not burn. Transfer to a small blender and add the ginger powder, salt, garlic, and vinegar. Blend until smooth. Add the olive oil and blend again to emulsify. Pour the dressing (to taste) over the bean mixture. Stir to coat and let sit for 15 minutes for the flavors to meld. The salad can also be covered and refrigerated for up to 3 days.

Recipe Notes

• For a quicker dish, use cracked freekeh instead. Cook it according to the package directions.

• Are you a spice lover? Add ½ a jalapeño pepper to the dressing before blending.

• Out of chickpeas? Any white bean can be substituted.

• No freekeh in the house? Try it with pearl barley instead.

Leek and Lemon Lentil Salad

▶ SOY-FREE POTENTIAL ▶ GLUTEN-FREE POTENTIAL

Because of their firm texture when cooked, French green lentils are one of our favorites for salads. Here we toss them with fresh crisp vegetables and a lightly-herbed leek dressing that will have you reaching for more.

1 cup (192 g) dry French green lentils

¼ cup (60 ml) olive oil

¾ cup (80 g) chopped leeks (white part only)

1 teaspoon dried thyme

2 cloves garlic, minced

¼ cup (60 ml) fresh lemon juice

1 teaspoon fine sea salt, or to taste

Pinch of ground black pepper, or to taste

1 carrot, peeled, cut into quarters, then thinly sliced

6 small radishes, cut into quarters, then thinly sliced

2 small sunchokes, cut into quarters, then thinly sliced

YIELD: 4 servings
PROTEIN CONTENT PER SERVING: 16 g

Bring a medium-size pot of water to a boil. Add the lentils. Reduce the heat to simmer. Cook for 25 to 30 minutes until tender. Drain and rinse with cold water. Drain again and then transfer to a medium-size bowl.

Heat the oil in a small skillet over medium heat. Add the leek and thyme. Cook, stirring occasionally, for 3 to 4 minutes until the leek is translucent. Add the garlic and cook for 1 minute longer. Transfer to a small blender. Add the lemon juice, salt, and pepper and process until smooth. Add the vegetables and dressing to the lentils. Stir to combine. Serve immediately or cover and refrigerate for up to 3 days. Taste and adjust the seasonings when serving.

Recipe Note

Sunchokes must be scrubbed well, but do not peel them before cutting. Not only is it awkward and dangerous, but many of the nutrients are in the skin. If you don't happen to have sunchokes, add an extra radish and part of a carrot to still keep the crunch.

Eat-It-Up Edamame Salad

▶ QUICK AND EASY

Bright and colorful foods are not only eye-catching, but also usually very palate-pleasing, too. The edamame pair well with their Eastern-cuisine counterparts to create a very satisfying salad.

2 cups (300 g) frozen, shelled edamame

3 ounces (85 g) somen noodles, broken into 1-inch pieces

Salt, for cooking

¾ cup (74 g) ½-inch (1.3 cm) pieces of snow peas

1 cup (70 g) thinly sliced baby bok choy

⅓ cup (27 g) minced scallion

½ cup (70 g) minced carrot

2 tablespoons (30 ml) seasoned rice vinegar

2 tablespoons (30 ml) tamari, or to taste

1 tablespoon (15 ml) vegetable broth

2 teaspoons ume plum vinegar (See Recipe Notes.)

2 teaspoons toasted sesame oil

½ teaspoon sambal oelek, or to taste

¼ teaspoon minced garlic

¼ teaspoon grated fresh ginger root

Salt and pepper

YIELD: 4 servings
PROTEIN CONTENT PER SERVING: 17 g

Bring a large pot of water to boil. Add the edamame, somen, and salt. Cook for 2 minutes or until the noodles are soft, but do not overcook. (See Recipe Notes.) Drain immediately and rinse under cold water until chilled, draining again. Combine the snow peas, baby bok choy, scallion, and carrot in a medium-size bowl. Add the somen and edamame to the vegetables.

Combine the rice vinegar, tamari, broth, ume plum vinegar, sesame oil, sambal oelek, garlic, and ginger in a small blender. Process until smooth. Pour over the salad and stir to coat. Cover and refrigerate for 1 hour, or longer for the flavors to meld. Taste and adjust the seasonings when serving.

Recipe Notes

• When substituting other types of pasta, follow the package directions and adapt the cooking time so it works with the edamame cooking time.

• Ume plum vinegar is a concentrated, salty vinegar with a very bold flavor profile. It can be found in the ethnic aisle of well-stocked grocery stores.

• This dish can be covered and refrigerated up to 3 days. If this is being prepared ahead of time, consider doubling the dressing recipe. Add the extra as needed.

BBQ Lentils

Baked lentils never tasted so good! Try serving them combined with cooked brown rice, quinoa, or baked potatoes. Add kale or spinach for a superbly healthy, filling, and fiber-rich meal.

2 cups (384 g) dried green lentils

4 cups (940 ml) water

2 teaspoons olive oil

½ cup (80 g) chopped red onion

3 medium carrots, peeled and trimmed, minced

½ cup (120 g) organic ketchup

¼ cup (66 g) tomato paste

½ cup (120 ml) water

¼ cup (60 ml) apple cider vinegar (See Recipe Note.)

2 tablespoons (30 ml) liquid smoke

2 tablespoons (40 g) agave nectar or pure maple syrup

2 tablespoons (30 ml) vegan Worcestershire sauce

2 tablespoons (30 g) Dijon mustard

1½ teaspoons onion powder

½ to 1 scant teaspoon fine sea salt, or to taste

⅛ to ½ teaspoon cayenne pepper, or to taste

YIELD: 8 to 10 servings

PROTEIN CONTENT PER SERVING: 12 g

Rinse the lentils and drain well. Pick through them to remove any stones or other debris. Place them in a large pot and cover with the water. Bring to a low boil over medium-high heat, and then reduce the heat to a simmer. Cook uncovered until tender but not mushy, about 30 minutes. Add water if necessary to make sure the lentils are barely covered. The cooking time will depend on the freshness of the lentils. Once cooked, drain and set aside.

Heat the oil in a medium skillet over medium-high. Add the onion and carrots, lower the heat to medium, and cover with a lid. Cook until tender, about 10 minutes, stirring occasionally.

Preheat the oven to 350°F (180°C, or gas mark 4).

In a 10-inch (25 cm) oven-safe dish, whisk to combine the ketchup, tomato paste, water, apple cider vinegar, liquid smoke, agave or maple syrup, Worcestershire sauce, mustard, onion powder, salt, and cayenne pepper. Add the cooked lentils and carrots and stir until they are coated with the sauce. Bake for 30 minutes until the sauce is slightly caramelized on the edges.

This dish can be covered and stored in the refrigerator once cooled for up to 5 days. It also freezes well for up to 3 months.

Recipe Note

This recipe makes for a bit of a zippy barbecue sauce, just the way we like it. So if you prefer taking it easy with the vinegar, switch to only 2 tablespoons (30 ml) of apple cider vinegar and increase the water to ½ cup plus 2 tablespoons (150 ml).

Beans and Greens Bowls

We've coated this wholesome bowl with delicious pepita pesto to make it taste more decadent than it actually is.

FOR THE PEPITA PESTO:

1 cup (40 g) packed fresh basil

½ cup (15 g) packed fresh baby spinach

¼ cup (30 g) roasted pepitas (hulled pumpkin seeds)

2 tablespoons (15 g) nutritional yeast

2 tablespoons (30 ml) extra-virgin olive oil

2 tablespoons (30 ml) vegetable broth, more if needed

1 tablespoon (15 ml) fresh lemon juice

1 to 2 cloves garlic, pressed or grated

Salt and pepper

FOR THE VEGGIES AND BARLEY:

Olive oil, to lightly brush pan

8 ounces (227 g) trimmed Brussels sprouts, quartered

12 ounces (340 g) small broccoli florets

½ cup (50 g) chopped scallion

⅓ cup (80 ml) vegetable broth, more if needed

9 ounces (255 g) cooked shelled edamame

One package (8.8 ounces, or 249 g) 10-minute barley (See Recipe Note.)

8 cups (2 L) vegetable broth

YIELD: 4 servings
PROTEIN CONTENT PER SERVING: 23 g

To make the pesto: Place the basil, spinach, pepitas, and nutritional yeast in a food processor. Process until finely chopped. Add the oil, broth, lemon juice, garlic, salt, and pepper. Process until combined, stopping to scrape the sides once. Set aside.

To make the veggies and barley: Lightly brush a large skillet with oil and heat on medium-high heat. Add the Brussels sprouts. Sauté for 4 minutes. Add the broccoli florets and scallion. Sauté until fragrant and slightly browned, another 4 minutes. Add the broth, stir to combine, and lower the heat to medium. Cover with a lid to cook until tender, about 4 to 6 minutes. Stir the veggies occasionally and add extra broth if needed.

Add the edamame and cook until warm, about 2 minutes.

Remove from the heat and stir in the pesto.

While the veggies are cooking, bring the broth to a boil in a medium saucepan. Add the barley, lower the heat to medium, and boil until al dente, about 10 minutes.

Drain and divide among 4 bowls. Divide the veggies among the bowls and serve immediately. Leftovers can be stored in the refrigerator in an airtight container for up to 3 days. Reheat on low heat in a skillet, adding extra broth if needed to keep this dish moistened.

Recipe Note

If you cannot find 10-minute barley (we buy it at Trader Joe's, here in the U.S.), use any grain in its place, and cook the chosen grain according to the directions on the package. Factor in between ½ cup and ¾ cup of cooked grain (weight will vary) per serving, depending on your appetite.

Butter Bean Crostini

▶ SOY-FREE POTENTIAL

Similar to a hummus, but in a more Mediterranean-style, we think you'll love this easy appetizer or side dish. With pine nuts for crunch and basil (just because . . . basil!), this protein spread has proven popular with all ages.

FOR THE SPREAD:

1 can (15 ounces, or 425 g) butter beans, drained and rinsed

2 sun-dried tomato halves, minced (moist vacuum-packed)

2 cloves garlic, peeled and sliced in half lengthwise

1 tablespoon (15 ml) dry white wine, or vegetable broth

4 sprigs fresh thyme

½ teaspoon herbes de Provence

2 teaspoons fresh lemon juice

1 tablespoon (9 g) capers, drained, and minced

Vegetable broth, or water, if needed

Salt and pepper

FOR THE CROSTINI:

2 tablespoons (30 ml) olive oil

½ teaspoon garlic salt

¼ teaspoon ground black pepper

16 (¼-inch, or 6 mm) slices of French bread

2 tablespoons (18 g) pine nuts

1 teaspoon nutritional yeast

3 tablespoons (8 g) slivered fresh basil

1 to 2 tablespoons (15 to 30 ml) good quality balsamic vinegar

YIELD: 16 crostini
PROTEIN CONTENT PER CROSTINI: 8 g

Preheat the oven to 400°F (200°C, or gas mark 6).

To make the spread: Tear an 18-inch (46 cm) piece of foil. Center the beans, sun-dried tomatoes, garlic, wine or broth, thyme, and herbes de Provence in a layer on the foil. Fold the foil to enclose the beans, forming a packet. Bake for 40 minutes until the garlic is roasted. Transfer to a medium-size bowl. Add the lemon juice and mash until smooth. If the mixture seems dry, add a splash of broth or water, as needed. Stir in the capers. Season to taste with salt and pepper.

To make the crostini: Combine the olive oil, garlic salt, and pepper in a small bowl. Brush the bread slices with the mixture on 1 side. Put them on a baking sheet, oiled-side up. Bake for 6 to 8 minutes. They should be lightly toasted but not dry.

Heat the pine nuts in a small skillet over medium heat. Cook, stirring, for 5 to 7 minutes, until toasted. Do not burn. Take them off the heat and stir in the nutritional yeast while they are still hot. Spread each crostini with 1 tablespoon (28 g) bean spread, a sprinkling of pine nuts, and a generous pinch of basil. Drizzle with a little balsamic vinegar and serve immediately.

Cacciatore Chickpea-Smothered Cauliflower Steaks

▶ SOY-FREE POTENTIAL ▶ GLUTEN-FREE POTENTIAL

Roasted cauliflower steaks are piled high with our tasty chickpea concoction in a way that is stunning to see—and a fantastically flavorful take on the dish. Sure, *cacciatore* means "hunter-style," but our gatherers' version more than hits the mark.

FOR THE CACCIATORE CHICKPEAS:

1 tablespoon (15 ml) olive oil

½ of a medium onion, cut into ½-inch (1.3 cm) slices

½ of a bell pepper (any color), cut into ½-inch (1.3 cm) slices

4 ounces (113 g) cremini mushrooms, cut into quarters

4 cloves garlic

1 teaspoon dried thyme

1 teaspoon dried basil

½ teaspoon dried rosemary

1½ cups (246 g) cooked chickpeas (See Recipe Note.)

1 can (14.5 ounces, or 411 g) diced tomatoes, undrained

1 teaspoon fine sea salt

½ teaspoon ground black pepper

2 tablespoons (8 g) minced fresh parsley

Minced fresh basil, for garnish

FOR THE CAULIFLOWER STEAKS:

1 large head of cauliflower

1 tablespoon (15 ml) olive oil

Salt and pepper

YIELD: 4 servings

PROTEIN CONTENT PER SERVING: 8 g

To make the chickpeas: Preheat the oven to 400°F (200°C, or gas mark 6). In a 9 x 13 inch (23 x 33 cm) glass baking dish, combine the oil, onion, bell pepper, mushrooms, garlic, thyme, basil, and rosemary. Roast in the oven for 30 minutes until the peppers and onions are slightly brown on the edges. Remove the garlic and mince. Add the garlic back to the mixture and stir in the chickpeas, diced tomatoes, salt, and pepper. Bake for 15 minutes. Stir in the parsley.

To make the cauliflower steaks: Cut the cauliflower as evenly as possible into four (1 inch, or 2.5 cm) slices, from the crown to the stem. Reserve the remaining florets for another purpose.

Line a large baking sheet with foil. Heat the oil in a large skillet over medium to medium-high heat. Cook the cauliflower steaks (in batches) for 4 to 6 minutes until browned. Gently turn the cauliflower over and cook the second side for 3 to 5 minutes until browned. Transfer to the foil-lined sheet. Repeat with the remaining cauliflower. Put in the oven and roast for 8 minutes or to the desired tenderness. Divide the chickpea mixture evenly over the cauliflower steaks and garnish with basil.

Recipe Note

We use canned chickpeas as much as the next bean-loving fiends, but in this case, homemade are the way to go. With such simple ingredients, it really makes a difference. Cook a big batch of beans and freeze them in portions so you can make easy dishes like this in a flash.

Eggplant Balela

▶ SOY-FREE POTENTIAL ▶ GLUTEN-FREE POTENTIAL

Balela is a refreshing bean salad from the Middle East. We made it even more interesting by throwing marinated eggplant into the mix. It's the perfect accompaniment to many of the dishes in this book, such as Baked Falafel (page 38), Mujaddara (page 44), Pudla (page 40), and more. The longer it gets to sit in the fridge, the more the flavors meld, and the more irresistible balela becomes.

To make the marinated eggplant: Combine the tahini, oil, lemon juice, vinegar, nutritional yeast, onion powder, harissa paste, garlic, cumin, and salt in a shallow pan. Brush a generous amount of this mixture on both sides and edges of each piece of eggplant and place in the shallow pan. Place the pan in the refrigerator for 1 hour to marinate.

Preheat the oven to 450°F (230°C, or gas mark 8). Place the slices of eggplant on a large rimmed baking sheet.

Bake for 8 minutes, flip the slices, and bake for another 6 to 8 minutes until tender and golden brown. Remove from the oven and set aside. Once cool enough to handle, cut the eggplant slices into ⅓-inch (8 mm) cubes.

To make the balela: In a large bowl, combine the oil, lemon juice, vinegar, onion, and garlic. Add the chickpeas, black beans, roasted bell pepper, tomato, mint, parsley, cubed eggplant, salt, ground pepper, and red pepper flakes to taste. Chill overnight and serve cold or brought back to room temperature. Leftovers can be stored in an airtight container for up to 4 days, and they get even better with each passing day.

FOR THE MARINATED EGGPLANT:

1 tablespoon (16 g) tahini

1 tablespoon (15 ml) olive oil

1 tablespoon (15 ml) fresh lemon juice

1 tablespoon (15 ml) white balsamic vinegar

1½ teaspoons nutritional yeast

½ teaspoon onion powder

½ teaspoon harissa paste, or to taste

1 clove garlic, grated or pressed

½ teaspoon ground cumin

Salt, to taste

1 small eggplant (a little over 10 ounces, or 280 g), trimmed, cut in two widthwise and then length-wise in ½-inch (1.3 cm) slices

FOR THE BALELA:

1 tablespoon (15 ml) extra-virgin olive oil

2 tablespoons (30 ml) fresh lemon juice

2 tablespoons (30 ml) white balsamic vinegar

⅓ cup (53 g) minced red onion

2 cloves garlic, grated or pressed

1½ cups (246 g) cooked chickpeas

1½ cups (258 g) cooked black beans

½ of a roasted red or yellow bell pepper, chopped

1 small tomato, seeded if desired, minced

3 tablespoons (18 g) minced fresh mint leaves

3 tablespoons (11 g) minced fresh parsley

Salt and pepper

Red pepper flakes, to taste

YIELD: 6 servings

PROTEIN CONTENT PER SERVING: 9 g

Butter Bean Gravy

▶ QUICK AND EASY ▶ SOY-FREE POTENTIAL

Celine pleads guilty to belonging to a household that doesn't really love mushrooms. If you do love them though, feel free to mince the rehydrated 'shrooms and add them to the gravy, before or after it is blended. If you don't add the mushrooms to the gravy, do not discard them! Put them to good use in Mushroom Bean Spread (page 62), or Mushroom Cashew Mini Pies (page 84).

1 ounce (28 g) dried shiitake or any other dried mushrooms

2 cups (470 ml) vegetable broth, boiling, divided, more if needed

1½ cups (288 g) cooked butter beans

2 tablespoons (30 ml) neutral-flavored vegetable oil

¼ cup (40 g) minced shallot or ⅓ cup (53 g) minced red onion

2 cloves garlic, grated or pressed

2 tablespoons (15 g) whole wheat pastry flour or (16 g) all-purpose flour

1½ tablespoons (12 g) nutritional yeast

¼ cup (15 g) packed fresh parsley or 1 packed tablespoon (3 g) fresh sage leaves, minced

Salt and pepper

YIELD: 3 cups (665 g), or 6 servings
PROTEIN CONTENT PER SERVING: 12 g

Place the dried mushrooms in a large bowl and cover with 1 cup (235 ml) of the boiling vegetable broth. Set aside for 15 minutes. Gently squeeze the broth out of the mushrooms, being careful not to discard the broth.

Top what remains of the soaking broth with enough extra broth to get a total of 1½ cups (355 ml). Add the butter beans to the broth and blend until smooth with an immersion blender. (You can either add the parsley before blending or just stir it at a later point. Blending it now will yield a more green-tinted gravy.)

Place the oil in a large skillet and heat on medium-high heat. Add the shallot and garlic. Sauté on medium heat until fragrant and the shallot is translucent, about 2 minutes.

Sprinkle the flour over the shallot and stir to combine. Add the nutritional yeast and stir to combine, cooking until the flour and yeast smell toasty, about 2 minutes. Using a whisk, slowly add the warm broth into the flour mixture, whisking constantly to keep the gravy smooth. Cook until slightly thickened, about 4 minutes, and add the parsley (if you haven't done so already) or sage. Switch to stirring with a wooden spoon and simmer until the gravy has thickened to your liking, another 2 to 4 minutes. Adjust the seasonings to taste. Remove from the heat and serve immediately with mashed potatoes, cooked grains, or steamed vegetables.

Store cooled leftovers in an airtight container in the refrigerator for up to 4 days and slowly reheat in a small saucepan before use.

Mushroom Bean Spread

▶ SOY-FREE POTENTIAL ▶ GLUTEN-FREE POTENTIAL

We prefer leaving this earthy, umami-rich, bean-based spread slightly chunky. Our favorite eating M.O. is to slather it on rustic whole-grain bread or crackers, like The Seed Crackers (page 78), for a great savory protein-packed snack. If you have a hard time finding affordable dried mushrooms, this recipe is a breeze to halve.

2 packs (0.88 ounces, or 25 g, each) dried mushroom mix of choice

2 cups (470 ml) vegetable broth, boiling

1 tablespoon (15 ml) toasted sesame oil

4 cloves garlic, grated or pressed

2 tablespoons (8 g) sun-dried tomato halves

1 teaspoon dried oregano

½ teaspoon red pepper flakes

1½ cups (246 g) cooked chickpeas or (266 g) cannellini beans

¼ cup (64 g) tahini

1 tablespoon (15 ml) olive oil

2 tablespoons (30 ml) liquid from jar of capers

2 tablespoons (30 ml) fresh lemon juice

2 teaspoons onion powder

2 tablespoons (18 g) capers, drained and minced

Salt and pepper

YIELD: 2 packed cups (560 g), or 8 servings
PROTEIN CONTENT PER SERVING: 4 g

Quickly rinse the dried mushrooms and place them in a medium bowl. Add the broth on top and soak for 20 minutes. Gently squeeze the liquid out of the mushrooms, without discarding it. It will be used when processing the spread and the leftovers can be stored in an airtight container in the refrigerator for up to 1 week to replace vegetable broth in any recipe.

Heat the oil in a large skillet on medium-high. Add the garlic, sun-dried tomatoes, mushrooms, oregano, and red pepper flakes. Lower the heat to medium and cook until lightly browned and fragrant, about 6 minutes, stirring occasionally.

Place the cooked mushrooms, chickpeas or cannellini beans, tahini, olive oil, caper liquid, lemon juice, and onion powder in a food processor. Process until slightly chunky. Add the capers and pulse a few times until the capers are mixed throughout the spread.

Add the mushroom-soaking broth as needed if the spread is too thick for your taste, 1 tablespoon (15 ml) at a time. Adjust the seasonings to taste.

Place in an airtight container in the refrigerator for at least 3 hours or overnight to let the flavors meld. Store leftovers in the refrigerator up to 4 days. Add additional mushroom-soaking broth if the spread is too thick for your taste after refrigeration, stirring to thoroughly combine.

3

GRAIN, NUT, AND SEED POWERHOUSES

Fuel Your Body with Some of Nature's Least Processed Bounty

We've got a thing for nature. We've also got a thing for fueling our bodies. That's why we love using versatile whole grains, nuts, and seeds to enhance the taste and texture of our recipes. These flavorful additions will make getting your protein a walk in the park.

Jump right in and explore the unlimited variations these nutritional powerhouses have in store for us! This chapter is full of delicious savory recipes and creative protein-packed ideas for breakfast, dessert, and, of course, snacks. Power up!

Gingerbread Quinoa Granola

▶ QUICK AND EASY ▶ SOY-FREE POTENTIAL

This scrumptious granola is loaded with protein from the cashew butter and quinoa flakes. The spicy gingerbread flavor gives you the perfect excuse to make something holiday-centric all year long. Happy breakfast to all and to all a good day!

½ cup (170 g) regular molasses

¼ cup (48 g) Sucanat

½ cup (128 g) cashew butter
or sunflower butter

1 teaspoon pure vanilla extract

¼ cup (60 ml) neutral-flavored oil

Scant ½ teaspoon fine sea salt

1½ teaspoons ground cinnamon

1 teaspoon ginger powder

½ teaspoon ground allspice

¼ teaspoon grated nutmeg

About 20 pieces (2.5 ounces, or 70 g)
of crystallized ginger, chopped small

2 cups (160 g) rolled oats

2 cups (204 g) quinoa flakes
(See Recipe Notes.)

YIELD: About 6 cups (770 g), or
12 servings

PROTEIN CONTENT PER SERVING: 6 g

Preheat the oven to 300°F (150°C or gas mark 2). Have a large rimmed baking sheet handy.

In a large bowl, combine the molasses, Sucanat, cashew butter, vanilla, oil, salt, spices, and chopped crystallized ginger. Stir to combine.

Add the oats and quinoa flakes on top. Stir to thoroughly coat.

Evenly spread the granola on the sheet and bake in 10-minute increments, carefully flipping the granola (see Recipe Notes) with a large wooden spatula after each increment, for a total of 20 to 25 minutes, until the granola looks dry and just slightly browned.

Let cool on the sheet. The granola will crisp up as it cools. Let cool completely. Store the cooled granola in an airtight container for up to two weeks, at room temperature or in the refrigerator.

Recipe Notes

• For the sake of clarity and awesome results, we're talking about quinoa flakes that look like quick-cooking rolled oats, *not* those that are similar to corn flakes. We use the Ancient Harvest brand.

• A good trick to getting big crumbles in your granola is to use a large wooden spatula. Lift the granola to flip it instead of stirring, so that the crumbles don't fall apart.

Sesame Berry Squares

When a snack attack sneaks up on us, we can't get enough of these little squares paired up with a cold glass of unsweetened coconut-almond milk. The good news is they're quite nutritious on top of being delicious—so thumbs way up if you feel like having seconds.

Nonstick cooking spray

¾ cup (240 g) all natural raspberry or strawberry jam

2 tablespoons (24 g) chia seeds

1⅓ cups (160 g) whole wheat pastry flour

¼ cup (40 g) hulled hemp seeds

¼ teaspoon fine sea salt

½ cup plus 1½ teaspoons (136 g) tahini

¼ cup plus 2 tablespoons (120 g) pure maple syrup

1 teaspoon pure vanilla extract

Plain or vanilla vegan milk, as needed

YIELD: 16 squares
PROTEIN CONTENT PER SQUARE: 3 g

Preheat oven to 350°F (180°C, or gas mark 4). Lightly coat an 8-inch (20 cm) square baking pan with cooking spray.

In a small bowl, combine the jam with the chia seeds and set aside. The seeds will expand a little and thicken up the jam while you prepare the crust.

Combine the flour, hemp seeds, and salt in a large bowl. Add the tahini, maple syrup, and vanilla on top, using a pastry cutter to stir them in. The dough must be moist without being too wet. It should stick together easily when pinched. If it is too dry, add 1 tablespoon (15 ml) of milk at a time until it is sufficiently moist.

Set aside a packed ½ cup (120 g) of the resulting dough.

Sprinkle the dough evenly in the prepared pan. Press it down evenly all over the bottom of the pan.

Cover with the jam mixture, spreading it all over with an angled spatula. Crumble the reserved dough on top, pressing slightly on top of the jam.

Bake for 24 minutes or until the crumbs on top are golden brown.

Place on a wire rack and cool for at least 30 minutes before slicing and serving.

Store leftovers in an airtight container at room temperature for up to 2 days.

Nuts and Seeds Breakfast Cookies

▶ QUICK AND EASY

These not-so-little nuggets of energy are composed of ingredients that make for a great (always too early) first meal of the day. The yogurt, cashew butter, hemp seeds, oats, and even whole wheat pastry flour all generously contribute to the protein bank, so that the need for a mid-morning snack becomes more unlikely.

6 tablespoons (72 g) Sucanat

2 tablespoons (40 g) pure maple syrup

¼ cup (60 g) plain or vanilla vegan yogurt or blended soft silken tofu

¼ cup (64 g) natural creamy cashew butter

2 tablespoons (30 ml) neutral-flavored oil

½ teaspoon pure vanilla extract

Scant ½ teaspoon fine sea salt

½ teaspoon ginger powder or ground cinnamon

⅓ cup (15 g) freeze-dried raspberries

3 tablespoons (30 g) shelled hemp seeds

1½ cups (120 g) old-fashioned oats

¾ cup (90 g) whole wheat pastry flour

½ teaspoon baking powder

YIELD: 8 big cookies

PROTEIN CONTENT PER COOKIE: 5 g

Preheat oven to 350°F (180°C, or gas mark 4). Line a large cookie sheet with parchment paper or a silicone baking mat.

In a large mixing bowl, combine the Sucanat, maple syrup, yogurt or tofu, cashew butter, oil, vanilla, salt, and ginger powder.

Add the berries, seeds, and oats on top. Sift the flour and baking powder on top.

Stir until well combined. Let stand for 5 minutes.

Scoop a packed ¼ cup (about 60 g) of dough per cookie onto the prepared sheet. Flatten slightly because the cookies won't spread a lot while baking. Repeat with the remaining 7 cookies.

Bake for 14 minutes or until the edges of the cookies are a light golden brown. Let cool on the sheet for 5 minutes before transferring to a cooling rack.

These are best served still warm from the oven or at room temperature. Store leftovers in an airtight container for up to 2 days.

Recipe Notes

• If cashew butter is a bit out of your budget, replace it with any other nut or seed butter you love.

• If you cannot find freeze-dried raspberries, replace them with chopped dried cherries, dried cranberries, or raisins.

Almonds Galore Pancakes

With all the almondy goodness they contain, we fell head over heels for these tender pancakes and luscious topping. We bet you will, too. The fact that almonds are one of the most protein-rich nuts one can munch on is a more than welcome added bonus.

FOR THE PANCAKES:

¾ cup plus 3 tablespoons (225 ml) plain or vanilla vegan milk

2 teaspoons apple cider vinegar

2 tablespoons (30 g) blended soft silken tofu, or plain or vanilla vegan yogurt

1 tablespoon (15 ml) neutral-flavored oil

1 tablespoon (20 g) pure maple syrup

1 teaspoon pure vanilla extract

1 teaspoon pure orange extract

¾ cup plus 3 tablespoons (113 g) whole wheat pastry flour

⅓ cup (40 g) almond meal

2 tablespoons (18 g) cacao nibs, optional

½ teaspoon baking powder

½ teaspoon baking soda

½ teaspoon ground cinnamon

Scant ¼ teaspoon fine sea salt

Nonstick cooking spray or oil spray

FOR THE TOPPING:

2½ tablespoons (40 g) natural creamy or crunchy almond butter

⅓ cup (107 g) pure maple syrup

Sliced almonds, for garnish

YIELD: 8 pancakes, plus ½ cup (120 ml) topping

PROTEIN CONTENT PER PANCAKE (WITH TOPPING): 6 g

To make the pancakes: Combine the milk and vinegar in a medium bowl. Let stand for two minutes to let the milk curdle. This is your "buttermilk."

Stir the blended tofu or yogurt, oil, maple syrup, and extracts into the buttermilk.

Combine the flour, almond meal, cacao nibs, baking powder, baking soda, cinnamon, and salt in a medium bowl. Stir the wet ingredients into the dry until just combined. Let stand for 5 minutes.

Heat a large nonstick skillet on medium-high heat. Lightly coat the skillet with cooking spray or oil spray away from the heat once it is hot enough to cook the pancakes.

Add ¼ cup (60 ml) of batter in the skillet. Spread the batter slightly with an angled spatula when adding it to the hot pan so that the pancakes cook fully. Cook on medium-low heat for about 3 minutes or until the center of the pancake bubbles.

Carefully flip the pancake and cook for another 2 to 3 minutes.

Repeat with the remaining pancakes. If you notice that your pancakes come out a little too dense, add a little extra milk as needed to thin out the batter.

While the pancakes are cooking, prepare the topping.

To make the topping: Combine the almond butter with the maple syrup. You will have to stir it again right before use. Drizzle some of the topping over the pancakes and garnish with sliced almonds.

Hearty Quinoa Waffles

We always have a batch or two of these healthy waffles at the ready in the freezer, waiting to be popped into the oven for breakfast, brunch, or "brinner" bliss.

1½ cups (355 ml) water, divided

⅔ cup (119 g) chopped dates

3 tablespoons (42 g) solid coconut oil

3 tablespoons (60 g) pure maple syrup

1½ teaspoons pure vanilla extract

1¾ cups (210 g) whole wheat pastry flour

1 cup (185 g) packed cooked white quinoa

¼ cup (48 g) chia seeds

1 teaspoon baking powder

1 teaspoon ground cinnamon

Generous ¼ teaspoon fine sea salt

Nonstick cooking spray

YIELD: 6 to 8 waffles

PROTEIN CONTENT PER WAFFLE: 7 g

Before starting, here's a quick note: It's best to make sure that all ingredients are at room temperature when making the batter so that the coconut oil doesn't solidify when combined.

Combine 1 cup (235 ml) of water and dates in a small saucepan. Bring to a boil, lower the heat, and cook on medium-high heat just until the dates start to fall apart; it should take about 2 to 3 minutes. Stir the coconut oil into the hot mixture to melt. Set aside to cool for at least 30 minutes. (Note that this can also be done in the microwave, using a deep, microwave-safe container and proceeding in 1-minute increments.)

Add the remaining ½ cup (120 ml) water, maple syrup, and vanilla, stirring to combine.

Place the flour, quinoa, chia seeds, baking powder, cinnamon, and salt in a large mixing bowl, stirring to combine.

Pour the wet ingredients onto the dry and stir until combined. Let stand while heating the waffle maker according to the manufacturer's instructions.

Lightly coat the waffle iron with cooking spray. Add ½ cup (135 g) waffle batter to two squares of the waffle maker or follow the manufacturer's instructions to fit just enough batter so that it doesn't overflow and so that the waffles get properly cooked.

Close the waffle iron and cook until dark golden brown, about 8 minutes. Remove the waffles from the iron and let stand at least 5 minutes on a cooling rack so that the waffles can crisp up. Do not miss this step!

Leftovers are even better: You can toast them in a toaster or toaster oven to crisp up the waffles again. You can also freeze the waffles for up to 3 months, as long as you wrap them up tightly. Throw them still frozen directly in the toaster or toaster oven until heated through and crisp.

Peanut Berry Muffins

We've kept these perfectly peanutty muffins moderately sweetened so that they can be served with extra jam on the side. Choose the jam that matches the berry you've used in the muffins or switch things up a bit—You rebel, you!

Nonstick cooking spray, if needed

1 cup (256 g) natural creamy or crunchy peanut butter

1 cup (235 ml) plain or vanilla vegan milk

⅔ cup (127 g) Sucanat

¼ cup (60 g) blended soft silken tofu, or plain or vanilla vegan yogurt

2 teaspoons pure vanilla extract

1½ cups (180 g) whole wheat pastry flour

2½ teaspoons baking powder

½ teaspoon fine sea salt

½ cup (23 g) freeze-dried raspberries or blueberries

All-natural raspberry or blueberry jam, for serving

YIELD: 12 muffins

PROTEIN CONTENT PER MUFFIN: 8 g

Preheat the oven to 350°F (180°C, or gas mark 4). Line a standard muffin pan with paper liners, or lightly coat it with cooking spray instead if using more berries. (See Recipe Notes.)

In a large bowl, whisk together the peanut butter, milk, Sucanat, tofu or yogurt, and vanilla to combine.

Sift the flour, baking powder, and salt on top of the wet ingredients. Stir the dry ingredients into the wet, being careful not to over mix. Gently fold in the berries.

Divide the batter into the muffin tin, filling each cup to a generous three-quarters if using paper liners or to just three-quarters without liners.

Bake for 22 minutes or until a toothpick inserted in the center of a muffin comes out clean. Place the muffins on a wire rack for about 15 minutes before serving. The muffins are best served freshly baked and still slightly warm, with optional jam on the side. Store cooled leftovers in an airtight container at room temperature for up to 2 days.

Recipe Notes

• If you want a larger amount of berries in your muffins (30 g in all instead of 23 g), it is preferable not to use paper liners and to coat the pan with nonstick cooking spray instead to get the same yield of 12.

• If you cannot find freeze-dried fruit, substitute ½ cup (65 g) fresh raspberries or (74 g) blueberries instead.

Quinoa Crunch Blueberry Muffins

▶ SOY-FREE POTENTIAL

It's true, the quinoa in the topping really is uncooked, giving these muffins an amazing crunch. We're happy to say that these were very warmly received by our testers. We frequently heard that these muffins excelled in both their healthfulness and their awesomeness! Here's hoping they are a hit with you and your family.

FOR THE TOPPING:

¼ cup (28 g) slivered almonds, chopped

2 tablespoons (22 g) dry quinoa

1 tablespoon (15 g) packed brown sugar

1 tablespoon (7 g) quinoa flour

1 tablespoon (15 ml) neutral-flavored oil

FOR THE MUFFINS:

½ cup (70 g) raw cashews

1¼ cups (295 ml) unsweetened plain vegan milk

2 tablespoons (14 g) ground flaxseed

2 teaspoons pure vanilla extract

3 tablespoons (45 ml) neutral-flavored oil

¾ cup (94 g) all-purpose flour

½ cup (56 g) quinoa flour

¼ cup (30 g) almond meal

¾ cup (170 g) packed brown sugar

1 tablespoon (8 g) cornstarch

2 teaspoons baking powder

1 teaspoon ground cinnamon

½ teaspoon fine sea salt

¼ cup (33 g) chopped dried apricots

¾ cup (109 g) fresh blueberries (See Recipe Note.)

YIELD: 12 muffins

PROTEIN CONTENT PER MUFFIN: 5 g

Preheat the oven to 375°F (190°C, or gas mark 5). Line a 12-cup muffin pan with paper liners.

To make the topping: Using a fork, stir together the almonds, quinoa, brown sugar, and quinoa flour in a small bowl. Add the oil and stir to combine. It will be a little crumbly.

To make the muffins: Blend the cashews, milk, ground flaxseed, and vanilla in a small high-powered blender until smooth. Add the oil and blend until combined, but do not emulsify.

Whisk together the flours, brown sugar, cornstarch, baking powder, cinnamon, and salt in a medium-size bowl. Stir in the apricots and blueberries. Pour the liquid ingredients into the dry ingredients and stir to combine. Do not overstir, but there should be no floury spots. Spoon about ¼ cup (72 g) of batter into each cup. Divide the topping evenly on the muffins, using about 2 teaspoons on each. Bake for 28 to 32 minutes until golden brown. Cool on a wire rack.

> **Recipe Note**
> If you'd prefer to use frozen blueberries, gently stir them into the batter right before scooping into the muffin cups.

Apple Pie Breakfast Farro

▶ SOY-FREE POTENTIAL

There's no shame in admitting that hot cereal usually isn't your cup of tea for breakfast. We're in the same boat actually, but we happen to be smitten with this cinnamon-flavored bowl. Let the apples retain some texture for the tastiest results.

8.8 ounces (249 g) quick-cooking dry farro

3 McIntosh apples, or any favorite apple, cored and chopped (about 18 ounces, or 510 g)

¼ cup (48 g) Sucanat or (38 g) light brown sugar (not packed)

1⅛ teaspoons ground cinnamon, plus optional extra for garnish

1 teaspoon pure vanilla extract

1 cup (235 ml) plain or vanilla vegan milk, warmed, as needed

1 or 2 recipes of nuts from Seed and Nut Ice Cream (page 93), or toasted nuts of choice

Pure maple syrup, optional

YIELD: 4 to 6 servings
PROTEIN CONTENT PER SERVING: 19 g

Bring a large pot of water to a boil. Add the farro and bring back to a boil. Lower the heat to medium-high and leave uncovered. Cook for 10 to 12 minutes until al dente or the desired consistency is reached. Drain and set aside.

Place the chopped apples, Sucanat or brown sugar, and cinnamon in the same large pot you used to cook the farro. Heat to medium-high, stirring to combine the ingredients. Once the apples start to release moisture, lower the heat to medium and cook until the apples are tender, about 10 to 15 minutes, stirring frequently. Note that the cooking time will vary depending on the size of the apple bits and what kind of apple you use. You're looking for tender bits, but not applesauce.

Remove the pot from the stove and stir the vanilla into the apples. Add the cooked grain into the apples and serve immediately, topping each serving with as much of the warm milk as desired. Top each serving with a handful of nuts, extra cinnamon, and maple syrup if desired.

Recipe Notes

• While quick-cooking grains usually retain less nutrition than their less processed counterparts, the total amount of uncooked farro used in this recipe still contains 30 g of protein. That's a pretty impressive amount for something prepared in a flash, and convenience is frequently key when whipping up a breakfast meal.

• You will need 3 generous cups (weight will vary for other grains) of cooked grain to prepare this dish: We prefer using grain that is al dente to get a nice texture and a nutty flavor. If you prefer a more tender grain, cook it to your own personal taste.

Raspberry Chia Breakfast Jars

We love serving this pudding-like, fruity treat in pretty glasses or jars for a light breakfast or snack. We also occasionally add a handful of our Gingerbread Quinoa Granola (page 64) on top, if we're feeling extra peckish. If you want to fancy things up a bit, a dollop of coconut whipped cream is also great.

12 ounces (340 g) frozen raspberries, thawed but not drained

12 ounces (340 g) soft silken tofu or unsweetened plain vegan yogurt

¼ cup (80 g) pure maple syrup

2 tablespoons (24 g) maple sugar or (30 g) light brown sugar, optional

¼ cup (48 g) white chia seeds

½ teaspoon pure vanilla extract

6 ounces (170 g) fresh berries (raspberries or blueberries), rinsed and thoroughly drained

YIELD: 6 servings

PROTEIN CONTENT PER SERVING: 7 g

Place the thawed raspberries in a blender or use an immersion blender to blend the berries until smooth. If you don't like berry seeds, pass the mixture through a fine-mesh sieve. Add the tofu or yogurt, maple syrup, and sugar to the berries and blend again until smooth. Place into a large bowl.

Stir the chia seeds and vanilla into the mixture. Cover and chill for at least 3 hours or overnight. Stir before serving.

Place a few of the fresh berries at the bottom of the serving dish. (You can also stir the berries directly into the mixture, keeping a few for garnishing.)

Divide the chia preparation on top and sprinkle with the remaining berries.

Leftovers can be stored in an airtight container in the refrigerator for up to 4 days.

Recipe Notes

• The results will be far richer, but you could use cashew cream (see page 91 for cashew base recipe) instead of tofu or yogurt to make this soy-free. Be sure to prepare it to the consistency of yogurt by adding extra water, if needed. It must also be super smooth.

• Adjust the quantity of extra sugar as needed. You could also simply use more maple syrup instead of (any) granulated sugar.

• Regular chia seeds are okay to use, but white chia seeds make for a prettier result.

Seed Crackers

▶ SOY-FREE POTENTIAL

Just when we thought there would never be a cracker we'd love more than our Cheezy Quackers (of *500 Vegan Recipes* fame), along came these crispy protein wonders! Make sure to cook your amaranth to a 1:1½ amaranth to water ratio to obtain a more pilaf-like seed than the porridge-like one a 1:3 ratio would yield. Follow the cooking instructions for amaranth in Crispy Amaranth Patties (page 88), if needed.

3 tablespoons (36 g) white chia seeds

⅓ cup (80 ml) water, more if needed

½ cup (120 g) packed cooked and cooled amaranth (See headnote.)

½ cup plus 2 tablespoons (75 g) whole wheat pastry flour, plus extra for rolling

3 tablespoons (30 g) shelled hemp seeds

3 tablespoons (23 g) golden roasted flaxseeds

2 tablespoons (15 g) almond meal

1½ teaspoons nutritional yeast

Generous ½ teaspoon fine sea salt

2 tablespoons (30 ml) olive oil

YIELD: About 100 crackers, or 20 servings
PROTEIN CONTENT PER SERVING: 2 g

Combine the chia seeds with the water in a small bowl. Let stand 2 minutes to thicken.

Place the amaranth, flour, hemp seeds, flaxseeds, almond meal, nutritional yeast, and salt in the bowl of a stand mixer. Add the thickened chia mixture and oil on top. Use a stand mixer fitted with a flat blade attachment to thoroughly combine. If the dough is crumbly or dry, add extra water, a few drops at a time. The dough should come together as a not-too-sticky ball. Shape the dough into a 5-inch (13 cm) disc; tightly wrap the dough in plastic wrap and refrigerate for 2 hours or overnight.

Preheat the oven to 400°F (200°C, or gas mark 6). Line two large baking sheets with parchment paper. Divide the dough into 4 portions.

Place a quarter of the dough on a lightly floured piece of parchment paper, lightly dust the top of the dough with flour, and roll out extremely thinly, about ¹⁄₁₆ inch (1.6 mm). Using a 2-inch (5 cm) round cutter, cut the dough into crackers and transfer to the prepared sheets. Roll out the dough scraps until you run out and repeat with the other 3 quarters of dough. You can also wrap the remaining dough tightly and place it back in the refrigerator for later use for up to 4 days.

Bake for 8 minutes and check for doneness: The crackers should be light golden brown all over. Some crackers are likely to bake faster than others; just remove those that are ready and transfer them onto a wire rack. Bake the rest until ready, in 1-minute increments, until light golden brown all over. Let cool on a wire rack before storing in an airtight container at room temperature. Leftovers should be enjoyed within 2 days.

Spelt and Seed Rolls

▶ SOY-FREE POTENTIAL

These tender, protein-packed rolls are perfect for spreading with nut butter or as a base for more creative sandwiches.

1 cup (235 ml) unsweetened plain vegan milk, lukewarm

2 teaspoons apple cider vinegar

½ cup (120 ml) water, lukewarm

2 tablespoons (30 ml) neutral-flavored oil

2 tablespoons (40 g) agave nectar or pure maple syrup or regular molasses

3 cups plus scant ½ cup (480 g) whole spelt flour, divided

¼ cup (30 g) oat flour or finely ground oats

¼ cup (36 g) vital wheat gluten

3 tablespoons (30 g) shelled hemp seeds

3 tablespoons (25 g) sunflower seeds

2 tablespoons (15 g) golden roasted flaxseeds

2 tablespoons (24 g) chia seeds

1 tablespoon (7 g) caraway seeds or (9 g) poppy seeds

1 teaspoon fine sea salt

2 teaspoons instant yeast

YIELD: 9 rolls

PROTEIN CONTENT PER ROLL: 15 g

Combine the milk and vinegar in a measuring cup. Let stand for two minutes to let the milk curdle. This is your "buttermilk."

Add the water, oil, and agave (or maple syrup or molasses) to the buttermilk. Set aside.

Place a scant 3¼ cups (450 g) of the spelt flour, the oat flour, vital wheat gluten, all the seeds, salt, and yeast in the bowl of a stand mixer. Pour the wet ingredients on top of the dry.

Knead for 10 minutes using a stand mixer fitted with a dough hook until the dough is pliable and soft without being too dry or too sticky. Slowly add extra water, 1 tablespoon (15 ml) at a time, if needed. (Alternatively, knead by hand on a lightly floured surface, for 10 minutes. Just add a scant ½ cup (60 g) less flour and add it in as you go, if needed.)

Cover and let rise 75 minutes or until doubled.

Punch down the dough. Place on a lightly floured baking sheet, flatten slightly, and shape into an approximately 10-inch (25 cm) round disk. Coat both sides of the disk with flour. Cut from the center into nine equal triangles, similar to scones. You can shape them into round buns, or leave them as is.

Gently shake off the excess flour and place the rolls back on the baking sheet. Flatten them slightly by pressing down gently with the palm of your hand. Cover with plastic wrap. Let rise 25 minutes.

While the rolls are rising, preheat the oven to 400°F (200°C, or gas mark 6). Remove the plastic wrap and bake for 20 to 22 minutes or until browned and hollow-sounding when tapped on the roll's underside. Let cool on a wire rack. Store leftovers in an airtight container at room temperature. The rolls are best enjoyed fresh, but will last for up to 2 days.

Nut and Seed Sprinkles

▶ QUICK AND EASY

▶ SOY-FREE POTENTIAL

▶ GLUTEN-FREE POTENTIAL

For an always-appreciated boost of flavor and protein, we recommend you add these sprinkles on top of pasta, Mean Bean Minestrone (page 26), or any Italian-inspired dish.

1 cup (145 g) toasted whole almonds

¼ cup plus 2 tablespoons (45 g) nutritional yeast

¼ cup (40 g) shelled hemp seeds

2 teaspoons white miso, or scant ½ teaspoon fine sea salt, to taste

1 to 2 cloves garlic, grated or pressed, to taste

1½ teaspoons favorite dried herb, or a blend (dried basil, dried oregano, dried thyme, dried parsley, Italian seasoning, herbes de Provence), optional

⅛ teaspoon cayenne pepper, or to taste, optional

YIELD: 2 cups (225 g), or 32 servings
PROTEIN CONTENT PER SERVING: 2 g

Place all the ingredients in a food processor. Pulse to combine until the almonds are coarsely ground to the consistency of panko bread crumbs.

Store in an airtight container in the refrigerator for up to 2 weeks.

Almond or Cashew Biscuits ▶

▶ QUICK AND EASY

These are nutty and buttery squares of perfection—ahoy!

1¼ cups (150 g) whole wheat pastry flour or (156 g) all-purpose flour

⅓ cup (47 g) toasted whole cashews or (48 g) almonds (Use unsalted.)

½ teaspoon fine sea salt

1½ teaspoons baking powder

3 tablespoons (42 g) semi-solid coconut oil (the texture of softened butter)

3 tablespoons (48 g) natural smooth cashew butter or almond butter

½ cup (120 g) blended soft silken tofu or unsweetened plain vegan yogurt

YIELD: 9 biscuits
PROTEIN CONTENT PER BISCUIT: 15 g

Preheat the oven to 425°F (220°C, or gas mark 7). Line a baking sheet with parchment paper.

Place the flour and nuts in a food processor. Pulse until the nuts are chopped: A few larger pieces are okay. Add the salt and baking powder and pulse a couple of times.

Add the oil and nut butter and pulse just to combine. Add the blended tofu or yogurt, and pulse until a crumbly (but not dry) dough forms. Gather the dough on a piece of parchment and pat it together to shape into a 6-inch (15 cm) square.

Cut into nine 2-inch (5 cm) square biscuits. Transfer the biscuits to the prepared baking sheet. Bake for 12 to 14 minutes, or until golden brown at the edges. Cool on a wire rack and serve.

Mushroom Cashew Mini Pies

Hemp powder is somewhat green-tinted, packed with protein, and has a subtly earthy flavor. We use the Nutiva brand, which also offers a high-fiber hemp powder. If you cannot locate hemp powder, feel free to replace it with the same amount of extra whole wheat pastry flour instead. The protein content will be lower, but the pies will still be delicious.

FOR THE FILLING:

1 scant cup (210 g) Creamy Cashew Baking Spread (page 92)

½ cup (80 g) minced rehydrated dried mushrooms of choice

¼ cup (15 g) chopped fresh parsley

2 tablespoons (20 g) minced red onion

2 tablespoons (15 g) nutritional yeast

2 cloves garlic, grated or pressed

¼ teaspoon fine sea salt

⅛ teaspoon ground nutmeg

Ground black or white pepper

FOR THE CRUSTS:

Nonstick cooking spray

1¼ cups (150 g) whole wheat pastry flour

¼ cup (40 g) hemp powder (See headnote.)

Scant ½ teaspoon fine sea salt

2 tablespoons (32 g) cashew butter

2 tablespoons (30 ml) neutral-flavored oil

¼ cup plus 2 tablespoons (90 ml) cold unsweetened plain vegan milk, as needed

YIELD: 24 mini pies

PROTEIN CONTENT PER PIE: 2 g

To make the filling: In a medium bowl, combine all the ingredients with a spoon until thoroughly mixed. Set aside while preparing the crusts.

To make the crusts: Preheat the oven to 350°F (180°C, or gas mark 4). Lightly coat a 24-cup mini muffin pan with cooking spray. Place the flour, hemp powder, and salt in a large bowl. In a small bowl, stir to combine the cashew butter and oil. Using a fork, cut the cashew butter mixture into the flour mixture. Add ¼ cup (60 ml) of the milk, stirring until crumbs form, adding an extra tablespoon (15 ml) at a time if needed. The crumbs of dough should stick together easily when pinched and be neither too dry, nor too wet.

Place a generous 1½ teaspoons of crumbs in each muffin cup, pressing down to fit the bottom and sides of the cup. Add 2 generous teaspoons of filling per crust, smoothing out the tops.

Bake for 22 minutes or until the tops are firm and light golden brown. Remove from the pan, transfer to a wire rack, and serve warm or at room temperature. Leftovers can be stored in an airtight container in the refrigerator for up to 2 days and reheated in a 325°F (170°C, or gas mark 3) oven until warm, about 15 minutes.

Farro-Stuffed Bell Peppers

▶ SOY-FREE POTENTIAL

We've packed colorful bell pepper halves with a protein-rich trifecta composed of farro, kale, and an irresistible cashew-based topping. If the tomatoes you use aren't very juicy, it will be necessary to add ½ cup (120 ml) of tomato sauce to the filling so that it is moistened enough to bake without getting dry. If you can only find regular farro, just follow the instructions on the package to cook it properly.

8.8 ounces (249 g) quick-cooking farro

4 cups (940 ml) vegetable broth

4 to 5 large bell peppers (each a little over 10 ounces, or 280 g), equally halved and trimmed

2 cups (134 g) packed kale leaves (no ribs)

¼ cup (15 g) fresh parsley

2 tablespoons (15 g) nutritional yeast

1 tablespoon (15 ml) olive oil

3 cloves garlic, pressed

5 ounces (140 g) chopped red onion

A little over 20 ounces (560 g) tomatoes, seeded if desired, diced (See headnote.)

1½ teaspoons dried oregano leaves

1 teaspoon dried thyme

1 teaspoon dried basil

½ teaspoon red pepper flakes, or to taste

½ teaspoon fine sea salt, or to taste

Ground black pepper

1 recipe Creamy Cashew Baking Spread (page 92)

YIELD: 8 to 10 stuffed bell pepper halves
PROTEIN CONTENT PER PEPPER HALF: 7 g

In a large pot, bring the broth to a boil. Add the farro and boil for 10 minutes, stirring occasionally. Drain well, place back in the large pot, and set aside.

Preheat the oven to 375°F (190°C, or gas mark 5).

Fit all the bell pepper halves in two 9 x 13-inch (23 cm × 33 cm) pans.

Place the kale, parsley, nutritional yeast, oil, and garlic in a food processor. Process until combined and finely chopped.

Stir the kale mixture into the drained farro along with the onion, diced tomatoes, oregano, thyme, basil, red pepper flakes, salt, and pepper until thoroughly combined.

If the bell pepper halves are large enough, you should be able to fit ¾ cup (150 g) of packed mixture in each half. Adjust as needed to fit the halves. (Note that filling leftovers can be simmered and enjoyed as is, if you run out of bell peppers.)

Cover the pans tightly with foil and bake for 40 minutes. Remove the foil and top each bell pepper half with 2 tablespoons (30 g) of Creamy Cashew Baking Spread. Bake for another 15 minutes, uncovered, until the spread is set and just slightly golden brown and the bell peppers are tender. Let cool for 10 minutes before serving.

Leftovers can be wrapped tightly once cooled and stored in the refrigerator for up to 3 days. Reheat in a preheated oven at 325°F (170°C, or gas mark 3) for 20 minutes or until heated through.

Wild Rice Pilaf with Spicy Cashews

We love to serve this already-protein-rich dish with one lightly browned, chopped sausage (Put More Protein In Your Sausages, page 142) stirred into the preparation during the last 4 minutes of cooking time.

FOR THE CASHEWS:

1½ teaspoons toasted sesame oil

1½ teaspoons agave nectar

1½ teaspoons tamari

1 teaspoon onion powder

1 teaspoon sriracha

¼ teaspoon garlic powder

¼ teaspoon ginger powder

1 cup (140 g) raw cashews

FOR THE PILAF:

1 cup (160 g) dry wild rice, rinsed

3 cups (705 ml) vegetable broth

2 teaspoons toasted sesame oil

12 ounces (340 g) carrots, trimmed, peeled, and cut into thin half-moons (about 5 carrots)

⅓ cup (53 g) minced shallot

3 cloves garlic, grated or pressed

3 tablespoons (45 ml) tamari

3 tablespoons (45 ml) fresh orange juice

1½ tablespoons (30 g) agave nectar

1½ teaspoons packed grated fresh ginger root or ½ teaspoon ginger powder

¼ to ½ teaspoon red pepper flakes, to taste

1 cup (150 g) steamed fresh English peas or thawed green peas

YIELD: 4 to 6 servings

PROTEIN CONTENT PER SERVING: 12 g

To make the cashews: Preheat the oven to 325°F (170°C, or gas mark 3). Combine the oil, agave, tamari, onion powder, sriracha, garlic powder, and ginger powder in a medium bowl. Add the cashews and stir to coat evenly. Place in an even layer on a parchment paper–lined rimmed baking sheet and bake for 8 minutes. Stir and bake for another 4 to 6 minutes until toasty and dry-looking, being careful not to let the nuts burn. Remove from the oven and let cool on the paper. Once cooled, use immediately or store in an airtight container in the refrigerator for up to 4 days.

To make the pilaf: Combine the rice and broth in a rice cooker. Cook until tender, about 40 minutes. Check for doneness and drain if ready. Add extra broth if needed.

In a large skillet, add the oil, carrots, and shallot and sauté on medium heat until the carrots are barely tender, about 10 minutes.

Combine the garlic, tamari, orange juice, agave, ginger, and red pepper flakes in a small bowl. Add ¼ cup (60 ml) of this mixture to the carrots, cover, lower the heat, and simmer until completely tender, about 6 minutes. Stir the wild rice and green peas into the carrots, add the remaining tamari mixture, and simmer for another 4 minutes. Stir the nuts into the rice mixture. Serve warm.

Leftovers can be stored in an airtight container in the refrigerator for up to 4 days and gently reheated.

Recipe Note

For a saucier dish, combine 1 tablespoon (15 ml) fresh orange juice with 1 tablespoon (20 g) agave nectar, and fold into the preparation after reheating.

Crispy Amaranth Patties

The whoopie pie pan used here makes for perfectly shaped patties that will be a beautiful golden brown—not to mention, crispy outside and tender and moist inside. If you don't have one, you can shape the mixture with moistened hands into 3-inch (7.5 cm) patties and bake the patties on a baking sheet lined with parchment paper.

1 cup (180 g) dry amaranth

1½ cups (355 ml) water

½ ounce (14 g) dry mushroom of choice

¾ cup (180 ml) vegetable broth, boiling

3 tablespoons (45 ml) fresh lemon juice

1 tablespoon (15 ml) olive oil

⅓ cup (53 g) minced red onion

2 cloves garlic, grated or pressed

1 tablespoon (8 g) nutritional yeast

½ teaspoon dried oregano

Scant ½ teaspoon dried basil

¼ teaspoon dried thyme

½ teaspoon fine sea salt

Ground peppercorn

¼ cup (30 g) whole wheat pastry flour or (31 g) all-purpose flour

2 tablespoons (16 g) cornstarch or arrowroot flour

1 tablespoon (12 g) chia seeds, optional

Nonstick cooking spray or oil spray

½ recipe Creamy Cashew Sauce (page 92), for dipping

YIELD: 12 patties

PROTEIN CONTENT PER PATTY: 5 g

Combine the water in a rice cooker with the amaranth and cook until the liquid is absorbed, about 20 minutes. (Alternatively, cook the amaranth on the stove top, following the directions on the package.) Let cool completely before preparing the patties.

Soak the mushrooms in the broth for 15 minutes. Gently squeeze out the liquid from the mushrooms once it is cool enough to handle, making sure not to discard the broth for use in other recipes (see page 18). Finely mince the mushrooms and set aside.

We like to use our stand mixer fitted with the paddle attachment for what follows, but it's not necessary. It just makes the preparation a little easier and less messy, as cooked amaranth is pretty sticky. In a large bowl, combine the cooled amaranth, mushrooms, lemon juice, oil, onion, garlic, nutritional yeast, oregano, basil, thyme, salt, and pepper. Add the flour, cornstarch or arrowroot, and chia seeds, stirring to thoroughly combine. Cover and refrigerate for at least 1 hour.

Preheat the oven to 400°F (200°C, or gas mark 6). Lightly coat a whoopie pie pan with cooking spray.

Use 3 packed tablespoons (about 55 g) of mixture for each patty, placing them on the pan; you will need to moisten your hands to help make the shaping easier as the mixture will be sticky. Flatten to fit the pan. Repeat with remaining mixture. You should get 12 patties in all.

Lightly coat the patties with cooking spray. Bake for 15 minutes, flip, coat with cooking spray again, and bake another 12 to 15 minutes until golden brown and firm. Let stand 10 minutes before serving warm or at room temperature with Creamy Cashew Sauce.

Broccoli and Mushroom Freekehzotto

▶ SOY-FREE POTENTIAL

We've taken the classic risotto and given it our own unique twist to create a comforting—yet elegant—dish that could grace a table in a five-star restaurant. Serve with baby greens lightly drizzled with your favorite dressing.

¾ ounce (21 g) dried chanterelle mushrooms (or dried mushroom of choice)

2 cups (470 ml) water, divided

2½ to 3 cups (590 to 705 ml) vegetable broth

2 tablespoons (30 ml) olive oil, divided

2 cups (142 g) very small broccoli florets

8 ounces (227 g) cremini mushrooms, chopped

1 cup (89 g) chopped leeks, white part only

1 cup (180 g) whole freekeh (See Recipe Note.)

½ cup (120 ml) dry white wine, or additional broth

5 cloves garlic, minced

1 teaspoon fine sea salt, divided

¼ cup (35 g) raw cashews

1 tablespoon (8 g) nutritional yeast

Salt and pepper

YIELD: 4 servings

PROTEIN CONTENT PER SERVING: 17 g

Recipe Note

Cracked freekeh can be substituted for whole freekeh. The cooking time will be 35 to 40 minutes. Follow the cooking cues instead of the timing.

Combine the chanterelle mushrooms and 1½ cups (355 ml) water in a small saucepan. Bring to a boil, and then reduce the heat to a simmer. Simmer for 10 minutes. Drain the mushrooms through a coffee filter, reserving both the liquid and the mushrooms. Add enough broth to the mushroom liquid to yield 4 cups (940 ml) of liquid. Rinse the saucepan and pour the broth water back into it. Bring to a very low simmer, just to keep warm. Rinse the mushrooms well, chop, and set aside.

Heat 1 tablespoon (15 ml) of the oil in a large skillet over medium heat. Add the broccoli and cook for 3 to 4 minutes until bright green, stirring occasionally. Add the cremini mushrooms and ½ teaspoon of salt. Cook for 3 to 4 minutes until the mushrooms are softened. Set aside.

Heat the remaining tablespoon (15 ml) of oil in a large, heavy-bottomed pot over medium-high heat. Add the leeks and freekeh and cook, stirring for 3 to 5 minutes, until the leeks are soft. Add the wine or additional broth, chanterelles, garlic, and salt and cook for 5 to 7 minutes, stirring until the liquid is absorbed by the freekeh (this is what makes it creamy). Add 1½ cups (355 ml) reserved broth/water mixture and stir until absorbed. Repeat this process.

Combine the cashews, nutritional yeast, and remaining ½ cup (120 ml) of water in a small blender. Process until completely smooth. Add this to the pot with the remaining cup (235 ml) of broth. Cook, stirring frequently, for about 1 hour. Most of the liquid should be absorbed and the freekeh should be tender. Stir in the cooked broccoli and cremini mushrooms. Taste and adjust the seasonings.

Cashew Raita

▶ SOY-FREE POTENTIAL ▶ GLUTEN-FREE POTENTIAL

Sure, you could make a simple raita from drained vegan yogurt, but it can be a bit of a struggle to find plain, unsweetened vegan yogurt these days. We use naturally soy-free cashews instead, making this raita version pretty divine. It's perfect for serving with Spicy Chickpea Fries (page 37), Split Pea Patties (page 32), Baked Falafel (page 38), Pudla (page 40), Mujaddara (page 44), and Tempeh Koftas (page 124). The cashew base for our raita is also used in the Simple Cashew Dip (page 124), which can be served with all of the recipes listed above, too.

FOR THE CASHEW BASE:

1½ cups (210 g) raw cashew pieces

¼ cup (60 ml) water, plus more to soak cashews, divided

¼ cup (60 ml) coconut cream (scooped from the top of an unshaken, chilled can of full-fat coconut milk stored in the refrigerator for 24 hours before use)

2 tablespoons (30 ml) fresh lemon juice

½ teaspoon fine sea salt

FOR THE RAITA:

1 English hothouse cucumber, cut into 6 large pieces

1 recipe (heaping 1½ cups, or 410 g) cashew base

3 tablespoons (5 g) packed fresh mint leaves

3 tablespoons (11 g) packed fresh parsley

3 tablespoons (3 g) packed fresh cilantro

1 to 2 cloves garlic, grated or pressed, to taste

½ teaspoon organic lemon zest

2 teaspoons to 1 tablespoon (10 to 15 ml) fresh lemon juice

Fine sea salt

YIELD: 21 ounces (585 g), or 12 servings

PROTEIN CONTENT PER SERVING: 6 g

To make the cashew base: Place the cashews in a medium bowl or four-cup (940 ml) glass measuring cup. Generously cover with water. Cover with plastic wrap, or a lid, and let stand at room temperature overnight (about 8 hours) to soften the nuts.

Drain the cashews (discard the soaking water) and give them a quick rinse. Place in a food processor or high-speed blender, along with ¼ cup (60 ml) water, coconut cream, lemon juice, and salt. Process until perfectly smooth, stopping to scrape the sides occasionally with a rubber spatula. This might take up to 10 minutes, depending on the power of the machine.

Transfer the spread into a medium bowl fitted with a lid or covered with plastic wrap and let stand at room temperature for 24 hours or until the spread smells tangy. This will depend on the temperature of your living area.

To make the raita: Place the cucumber in a food processor and pulse a few times to chop. Add the remaining ingredients and pulse until thoroughly combined, stopping to scrape the sides with a rubber spatula once or twice. Adjust the seasonings as needed. Place in the refrigerator for at least 2 hours, or overnight, to let the flavors meld. Gently fold again before serving. Leftovers can be stored in the refrigerator in an airtight container for up to 4 days.

Creamy Cashew Sauce

▶ GLUTEN-FREE POTENTIAL

This slightly cheesy sauce is amazing as a topping for dishes that will be baked, like The Whole Enchilada (page 42), or any favorite vegan lasagna recipe. It can also be used as is to coat pasta or grains, or with our Smoky Bean and Tempeh Patties (page 117), or Split Pea Patties (page 32).

1 cup (140 g) raw cashews (covered with water, soaked 8 hours, drained, rinsed)

1 cup (235 ml) vegetable broth

2 tablespoons (30 ml) fresh lemon juice

1 tablespoon (18 g) white miso

1½ tablespoons (12 g) cornstarch

1 teaspoon onion powder

Salt and pepper

YIELD: Scant 2 cups (440 ml) sauce, or 8 servings
PROTEIN CONTENT PER SERVING: 2 g

Combine all the ingredients in a blender, and blend until perfectly smooth. Add to a medium saucepan, and cook on medium-low heat until thickened, whisking constantly, about 3 minutes.

Remove from the heat, and whisk occasionally to avoid having a "skin" form on top of the mixture. Adjust seasoning as needed. Use immediately, or store in an airtight container in the refrigerator for up to 4 days.

Creamy Cashew Baking Spread

▶ SOY-FREE POTENTIAL

▶ GLUTEN-FREE POTENTIAL

Use the following superbly simple spread as a topping for baked dishes, like our Farro-Stuffed Bell Peppers (page 85), and as part of the filling for our Mushroom Cashew Mini Pies (page 84).

1 cup (140 g) raw cashews (covered with water, soaked 8 hours, drained and rinsed)

½ cup (120 ml) vegetable broth

1 tablespoon (15 ml) fresh lemon juice

YIELD: 10 ounces (283 g) baking spread
PROTEIN CONTENT PER SERVING: 26 g

Combine the cashews, broth, and lemon juice in a food processor or high-speed blender. Process until thoroughly smooth, stopping to scrape the sides occasionally. This might take up to 10 minutes depending on the efficiency of your food processor or blender.

Place in a glass bowl and cover tightly. Leave at room temperature for 24 hours or until the spread smells tangy. This will depend on the temperature of your living area. Store in the refrigerator after that, for up to 1 week.

Seed and Nut Ice Cream

▶ GLUTEN-FREE POTENTIAL

We know you will have a hard time resisting this protein-rich after-meal (or in-between-meal) treat. So don't!

FOR THE NUTS:

1½ tablespoons (30 g) pure maple syrup

½ teaspoon ground cinnamon

⅛ teaspoon ground nutmeg

⅛ teaspoon fine sea salt

½ cup (50 g) walnut or pecan halves

FOR THE ICE CREAM:

½ cup (128 g) tahini

½ cup (128 g) natural creamy cashew butter or peanut butter

12 ounces (340 g) soft silken tofu, or plain or vanilla vegan yogurt

½ cup plus 2 tablespoons (200 g) agave nectar or ¾ cup (240 g) pure maple syrup, more if needed

¼ cup (60 ml) full-fat coconut milk

½ teaspoon ginger powder

½ teaspoon ground cinnamon

1½ teaspoons pure vanilla extract

YIELD: 1 quart (950 ml), or 8 servings

PROTEIN CONTENT PER SERVING: 9 g

To make the nuts: Preheat the oven to 325°F (170°C, or gas mark 3).

In a medium bowl, combine the maple syrup, cinnamon, nutmeg, and salt. Add the walnut or pecan halves and stir to coat. Place in an even layer on a parchment paper-lined rimmed baking sheet and bake for 8 minutes. Stir and bake for another 4 to 6 minutes until toasty and dry-looking, being careful not to let the nuts burn. Remove from the oven and let cool completely before coarsely chopping them. Set aside.

To make the ice cream: Freeze the tub of your ice cream maker for at least 24 hours.

Place all the ingredients in a blender and blend until perfectly smooth. Taste a bit of the mixture to make sure it is sweetened enough to your taste and add more sweetener if desired, 1 tablespoon (15 ml) at a time. Blend again if you made adjustments.

Transfer the mixture to an ice cream maker and follow the instructions to prepare the ice cream. Add the chopped nuts during the last 5 minutes of churning. Transfer to a container and freeze for 2 hours to firm up. The ice cream will be reluctant to be scooped out straight out of the freezer after more than few hours, so leave it at room temperature for about 15 mnutes before serving.

Recipe Notes

• To keep your ice cream scoopably soft, add 2 tablespoons (30 ml) of dark rum and ¼ teaspoon xanthan gum into the mix while blending it all together.

• Note that maple syrup is less sweet than agave, so it might need to be increased according to taste. Dip a finger in the preparation before churning it, and adjust the amount of syrup (or nectar) to taste.

• If you're not a tahini fan, replace it with another seed or nut butter.

No-Bake Choco Cashew Cheesecake

▶ SOY-FREE POTENTIAL   ▶ GLUTEN-FREE POTENTIAL

A chocolaty, creamy filling surrounded by a no-bake crust makes for a luscious dessert that is a breeze to prepare. This cheesecake is also sophisticated enough for the most special occasions, especially when cut into tiny slices and topped with berry coulis (see Recipe Note), a little whipped coconut cream, and a few cacao nibs.

2 cups (280 g) raw cashews (covered with water, soaked 8 hours, drained, and rinsed)

¼ cup (60 ml) coconut cream (scooped from the top of an unshaken, chilled can of full-fat coconut milk stored in the refrigerator for 24 hours before use)

¼ cup (20 g) unsweetened cocoa powder

½ cup (160 g) pure maple syrup

1 teaspoon vanilla extract

1¼ cups (125 g) walnut halves

½ cup (89 g) chopped dates

½ teaspoon ground cinnamon

¼ cup (30 g) almond meal, as needed

YIELD: 8 to 12 servings
PROTEIN CONTENT PER SERVING: 9 g

Line the bottom of four 4-inch (10 cm) spring-form pans with a parchment paper circle.

Place the cashews, coconut cream, cocoa powder, maple syrup, and vanilla in a food processor or high-speed blender. Process until completely smooth, occasionally stopping to scrape the sides of the machine with a rubber spatula. Depending on the efficiency of your machine, this could take up to 10 minutes. Transfer the mixture into a medium bowl and set aside. Wipe the food processor or blender clean with a piece of paper towel.

Place the walnuts, dates, and cinnamon in the same food processor or high-speed blender. Process to chop finely and combine until the mixture sticks together when pressed. Be careful not to overprocess or the mixture will become too sticky. If it's too late and the mixture is too sticky, pulse the almond meal into the mixture. Press down into the prepared pans. Place the cashew mixture in the crust and smooth out the top. Place the pans in an airtight container in the freezer for 3 hours until set (this will make what follows less messy), remove the cheesecakes from the pans, and transfer back into the refrigerator until ready to eat.

Recipe Note

Serve this cheesecake topped with a simple coulis: Combine 12 ounces (340 g) frozen raspberries or strawberries and 2 tablespoons (40 g) pure maple syrup in a small saucepan and cook on medium heat until the berries fall apart, about 10 minutes. If you don't like seeds, strain through a fine-mesh sieve before using. This yields approximately 1½ cups (355 ml).

Cacao-Coated Almonds

▶ QUICK AND EASY ▶ SOY-FREE POTENTIAL ▶ GLUTEN-FREE POTENTIAL

While we're big fans of plain roasted almonds, we also love to dress them up a bit occasionally when we have a hankering for it. Ground cacao nibs provide these crunchy almonds with a depth of flavor that's hard to obtain from any other cocoa source. The espresso powder, while entirely optional, kicks it up another notch. We find the almonds look prettier with the addition of powdered sugar, but they're great when left without, too.

¼ cup (35 g) cacao nibs

¼ cup (38 g) light brown sugar (not packed)

1 teaspoon instant espresso powder, optional

Pinch of kosher salt

2 teaspoons cornstarch

2 teaspoons warm water

1 tablespoon (20 g) pure maple syrup

1 teaspoon pure vanilla extract

2 cups (240 g) roasted whole almonds

¼ cup (30 g) powdered sugar, optional

YIELD: 2½ cups (320 g) almonds, or 10 servings

PROTEIN CONTENT PER SERVING: 7 grams

Preheat the oven to 325°F (170°C, or gas mark 3). Have a large rimmed baking sheet lined with parchment paper handy.

Place the cacao nibs, sugar, espresso powder, and salt in a coffee grinder. (Do this in a couple of batches if your coffee grinder is small.) Grind to turn into a fine powder. In a large bowl, whisk the cornstarch with the warm water until thoroughly combined. Stir the maple syrup and vanilla into the mixture. Add the almonds on top and fold until thoroughly coated.

Add the ground cacao mixture and combine until the almonds are thoroughly coated.

Place the almonds evenly on the baking sheet. Toast for 10 minutes. Remove from the oven and stir gently. Toast for another 5 minutes or until the coating looks mostly dry. Be careful not to allow to burn!

Let cool on the sheet. The coating will further harden once cooled. Once completely cooled, place the nuts in a bowl or Ziploc bag and dust with the sugar, shaking to coat completely. Store in an airtight container in the refrigerator for up to 2 weeks.

Recipe Note

To roast the almonds, heat a nonstick pan on medium-high. Add the raw almonds and stir constantly for about 7 minutes until fragrant. Turn off the heat, leave the pan on the stove, and keep on stirring for 2 minutes. Transfer the nuts to a steel colander so that they can cool down uniformly.

4

TERRIFIC TOFU AND TEMPEH

Talk Soy to Me!

Sometimes thought of as "hippie foods," protein-packed tofu and tempeh are the perfect canvas for creating versatile and satisfying dishes, as their "naked" flavor is quite bland on its own. They are also complete proteins and widely available in the refrigerated section of most grocery stores. We always keep some tofu pressing (see page 15) in our refrigerators. It shares the shelf with marinating tempeh or tofu for fantastically fast meals. This chapter is filled with some of our favorites, both old and new!

Do the Cocoa Shake

▶ QUICK AND EASY ▶ GLUTEN-FREE POTENTIAL

Like many kids around the world, Celine used to drink more than her fair share of chocolate milk back in the day. She was (maybe a little too) excited to find out that this concoction tastes just as rich and swoon-worthy as the non-vegan beverage she grew up on.

12 ounces (340 g) soft silken tofu

1½ cups (355 ml) unsweetened plain or vanilla vegan milk of choice

¼ cup (80 g) agave nectar or pure maple syrup, adjust to taste

¼ cup (64 g) natural creamy peanut or almond butter, slightly salted is fine

¼ cup (20 g) unsweetened cocoa powder

1 teaspoon pure vanilla extract

2 tablespoons (20 g) hemp powder, optional

1 frozen banana (peeled prior to freezing in a plastic sandwich bag), optional

Ice cubes, optional

YIELD: 4 servings, 1 cup (235 ml) per serving
PROTEIN CONTENT PER SERVING: 11 g

Combine all the ingredients in a blender and blend until perfectly smooth. Add hemp powder for an extra boost of protein, a sliced frozen banana for a thicker and fruitier shake, or ice cubes for a colder, thicker shake without any added flavor. Serve immediately or refrigerate for later use: Just be sure to only add the ice cubes upon serving, if storing for later. Stir well or blend again if adding ice cubes.

Recipe Notes

• If there are nut or seed butters you favor more than peanut butter, you're welcome to use them in its place.

• Throwing a banana in the blender together with the other ingredients will, of course, add a banana flavor and help thicken the shake. Using ice cubes instead will also help thicken the shake without adding any possibly unwanted flavor.

• Hemp powder is a fantastic way to boost the protein profile of this shake, but its earthy flavor and texture might take a little bit of getting used to.

Veggie Sausage Frittata

The following frittata is one of those awesome dishes that tastes even better when reheated (you know the kind), which makes it perfect for breakfast throughout the week. Prepare it during the weekend, when you hopefully have more time to cook, and reheat it as noted below every morning of the week for a quick and filling breakfast.

3 tablespoons (45 ml) olive oil, divided

1 red bell pepper, cored and diced

½ cup (80 g) chopped red onion

4 cloves garlic, minced

1 Smoky Sausage (page 140), chopped into bite-size pieces

1 teaspoon smoked paprika

½ teaspoon ground cumin

1 pound (454 g) extra-firm tofu, drained

6 tablespoons (90 ml) vegetable broth

1 teaspoon liquid smoke

1 tablespoon (15 g) Dijon mustard

6 tablespoons (45 g) nutritional yeast

3 tablespoons (23 g) chickpea flour

3 tablespoons (24 g) cornstarch or arrowroot powder

1½ teaspoons onion powder

½ teaspoon ground black pepper, or to taste

¼ teaspoon turmeric

¼ teaspoon fine sea salt

¼ teaspoon black salt (or use another ¼ teaspoon fine sea salt)

Nonstick cooking spray

YIELD: 6 to 8 servings

PROTEIN CONTENT PER SERVING: 29 g

Place 1 tablespoon (15 ml) of oil in a large pot. Add the bell pepper, onion, and garlic and sauté on medium heat for 2 minutes. Add the sausage, paprika, and cumin. Stir and cook for another minute until the vegetables are barely tender. Remove from heat and set aside. This can also be done the night before and stored in the refrigerator in an airtight container once cooled.

Place the tofu, broth, remaining 2 tablespoons (30 ml) oil, liquid smoke, and mustard in a food processor. Process until smooth, stopping to scrape sides with a rubber spatula at least once. Add the nutritional yeast, flour, cornstarch or arrowroot, onion powder, black pepper, turmeric, and salts. Process until smooth, stopping to scrape sides with a rubber spatula at least once.

Place the cooked vegetable and sausage mixture in a large bowl. Scrape the tofu mixture on top and gently fold to combine.

Preheat the oven to 350°F (180°C, or gas mark 4). Lightly coat a 9-inch (23 cm) round baking pan or two 6-inch (15 cm) round baking pans with cooking spray. Scrape the frittata mixture evenly into the pan or divide it equally between the two smaller pans.

Bake the larger pan for 45 minutes or until set and golden brown on top. The smaller pans will only require about 30 minutes of baking, or until set and golden brown on top.

Remove from the oven and let stand 10 minutes before serving.

Leftovers can be wrapped tightly once cooled and stored in the refrigerator for up to 4 days. Reheat in a preheated oven at 325°F (170°C, or gas mark 3) for 15 minutes or until heated through.

High Brow Hash

▶ QUICK AND EASY

With homemade sausage, fingerlings, and fresh herbs, we think of this as one classy hash. But, truth be told, you can also make this dish to clean out the refrigerator: Just use whatever vegetables and herbs you have on hand. We like to use a cast-iron skillet because the residual heat gently cooks the garlic and warms the fresh herbs.

2 tablespoons (30 ml) olive oil

1 pound (454 g) fingerling potatoes, cut into ½-inch (1.3 cm) dice

½ of a Smoky Sausage (page 140), cut into ½-inch (1.3 cm) dice

½ cup (75 g) diced red or yellow bell pepper

¾ cup (75 g) small cauliflower florets

1½ cups (132 g) Brussels sprouts, thinly sliced

½ to 1 cup (120 to 235 ml) vegetable broth, as needed

⅔ cup (107 g) chopped shallot

1 cup (70 g) chopped mushrooms (any kind)

1 teaspoon fine sea salt

½ teaspoon ground black pepper

2 cloves garlic, minced

1 tablespoon (15 ml) fresh lemon juice, optional

2 tablespoons (6 g) minced fresh chives

1 tablespoon (2 g) minced fresh thyme

YIELD: 4 to 6 servings
PROTEIN CONTENT PER SERVING: 16 g

Heat the oil in a large skillet over medium heat. Add the potatoes and cook for 10 to 12 minutes, stirring occasionally, until browned. Add the sausage and cook for 5 to 7 minutes until browned. Add the bell pepper, cauliflower, and Brussels sprouts. Cook for 4 to 6 minutes until the vegetables are bright and just tender. Add a splash of broth if the vegetables are sticking and continue to do so, if needed. Add the shallot, mushrooms, salt, and pepper. Cook for 3 minutes until the shallot are cooked. Turn off the heat. Stir in the garlic, lemon juice, and fresh herbs. Taste and adjust the seasonings.

Recipe Notes

• Store-bought vegan sausage can be substituted for the homemade, if desired.

• For a potentially gluten-free dish, the sausage can also be omitted.

Tempeh Breakfast Stacks

Although we call this a breakfast stack, it also makes a terrific, quick-and-easy dinner if you've marinated the tempeh ahead of time.

3 tablespoons (45 ml) vegetable broth

3 tablespoons (45 ml) dry white wine, or additional broth

2 tablespoons (30 ml) tamari

2 teaspoons liquid smoke

4 teaspoons (27 g) pure maple syrup, divided

4 teaspoons (20 g) Dijon mustard, divided

1 teaspoon organic ketchup

½ teaspoon toasted sesame oil

Salt and pepper

8 ounces (227 g) tempeh, simmered, (page 15) cut in half laterally, then vertically to make 4 patties

2 tablespoons (30 ml) olive oil

2 tablespoons (20 g) minced onion

¼ cup (56 g) vegan mayonnaise

2 tablespoons (15 g) nutritional yeast

1 to 2 tablespoons (15 to 30 ml) white wine vinegar

High heat neutral-flavored oil, for cooking

2 English muffins, split and toasted

2 cups (40 g) baby arugula, divided

8 (½ -inch, or 1.3 cm) slices of tomato

YIELD: 4 servings, plus ⅓ cup (80 ml) sauce

PROTEIN CONTENT PER SERVING (WITH SAUCE): 19 g

Combine the broth, wine (if using), tamari, liquid smoke, 2 teaspoons each of the maple syrup and mustard, ketchup, and sesame oil in an 8 x 11 inch (20 x 28 cm) dish. Stir to combine and season with salt and pepper. Marinate the tempeh for 1 hour, or up to 24 hours, refrigerated.

Heat the olive oil in a small skillet over medium heat. Cook the onion for 3 to 5 minutes until translucent. Transfer to a small blender and add the mayonnaise, nutritional yeast, 1 tablespoon (15 ml) vinegar, and the remaining 2 teaspoons each of maple syrup and mustard. Process until smooth. Taste and add the additional vinegar, if desired. Process again. Return the sauce to the small skillet: the residual heat should keep it warm. If not, heat very gently over low heat. Season to taste with salt and pepper.

Heat a thin layer of oil in a large skillet over medium-high heat. Carefully put the tempeh in the skillet to cook. It may spatter. Cook for 3 to 5 minutes until browned. Turn over to cook the second side, for 3 to 5 minutes, until also browned.

Put an English muffin on each plate and top with ½ cup (10 g) of baby arugula, 1 tempeh patty, and 2 slices of tomato. Lightly sprinkle salt and pepper on the tomatoes. Drizzle with the sauce and serve.

Green Dip

▶ GLUTEN-FREE POTENTIAL

Fresh herbs add a bounty of flavor to this silken tofu and avocado dip. It's a quick way to get a protein fix in an unexpected place: as a vegetable or chip dip. Try it spread on sandwiches, too.

12 ounces (340 g) extra-firm silken tofu

2 avocados, pitted, peeled, and chopped

1 cup (100 g) chopped scallion

1 cup (160 g) chopped onion

¼ cup (60 ml) fresh lemon juice

4 cloves garlic, minced

1 tablespoon plus 1 teaspoon (11 g) nutritional yeast

¼ cup plus 2 tablespoons (24 g) chopped fresh dill

2 tablespoons (6 g) chopped fresh chives

2 teaspoons seasoned salt

2 teaspoons agave nectar

2 teaspoons prepared yellow mustard

2 teaspoons hot sauce

½ teaspoon ground black pepper

1 cup (20 g) packed fresh baby arugula

YIELD: 2½ cups (740 g) dip, or 10 servings
PROTEIN CONTENT PER SERVING: 4 g

Combine the tofu, avocados, scallion, onion, lemon juice, garlic, and nutritional yeast in a small blender or food processor. Process until smooth. Add the dill, chives, salt, agave, mustard, hot sauce, and pepper. Process until smooth. Add the arugula and pulse a few times to chop. Let sit for 1 hour for the flavors to meld. Taste and adjust the seasonings.

Serve with toasted baguette slices or raw vegetables.

Recipe Notes

• For a tortilla chip dip, substitute minced fresh cilantro for the dill and use lime juice instead of lemon juice.

• If desired, this recipe is easily halved. The remaining tofu can be used to prepare the Shishito Peppers with Peanut-Tofu Sauce (page 106).

Shishito Peppers with Peanut-Tofu Sauce

▶ QUICK AND EASY ▶ GLUTEN-FREE POTENTIAL

Shishito peppers are small, thin-skinned Japanese peppers. They are unique in that most are mild, but on average 1 out of 10 has a serious kick! The peppers are seasonal and a bit of a gourmet ingredient. We've found them packed in small tubs under the Melissa's label and occasionally at farmers' markets. Padron peppers can be substituted.

6 ounces (170 g) extra-firm silken tofu, drained

3 tablespoons (48 g) smooth or chunky peanut butter

3 tablespoons (45 ml) seasoned rice vinegar

2 tablespoons (30 ml) tamari

1 teaspoon garlic powder

1 teaspoon onion powder

½ teaspoon ginger powder

1 to 3 teaspoons (5 to 15 g) sriracha, or to taste

2 teaspoons olive oil

4 ounces (113 g) shishito peppers (about 20 peppers)

2 tablespoons (12 g) minced scallion

1 tablespoon (9 g) chopped dry-roasted peanuts

2 teaspoons toasted sesame seeds

Coarse sea salt, for sprinkling

YIELD: About 20 peppers, plus 1 generous cup (300 g) Peanut-Tofu Sauce

PROTEIN CONTENT PER PEPPER (WITH SAUCE): 33 g

Combine the tofu, peanut butter, vinegar, tamari, garlic powder, onion powder, and ginger powder in a small blender. Process until completely smooth. Add sriracha to taste and blend again.

Heat the oil in a large skillet over medium-high heat. Cook the peppers for 4 to 6 minutes, turning occasionally, until there are a few black spots and blisters. Transfer to a plate and spoon as much sauce as desired over the peppers, serving some extra on the side. Sprinkle with the scallion, peanuts, sesame seeds, and salt.

Recipe Note

You'll probably have extra tofu sauce. It can be stored airtight in the refrigerator for up to 3 days. It makes a tasty salad dressing and is wonderful drizzled on steamed vegetables, such as broccoli. Or use it as a sauce for a rice bowl, or even quickie peanut noodles.

Fiesta Scramble

▶ QUICK AND EASY ▶ GLUTEN-FREE POTENTIAL

If scrambled eggs used to be among your favorite foods to enjoy at least once a day, don't despair: Tofu scrambles have come a long way, and will be just as delicious and satisfying when prepared properly. Let us show you the ropes.

2 tablespoons (30 ml) olive oil

1 pound (454 g) super firm tofu, crumbled

½ teaspoon turmeric

½ teaspoon ground cumin

½ teaspoon black salt, optional

¼ cup (30 g) nutritional yeast

⅓ cup (33 g) chopped scallion

2 tablespoons (20 g) chopped red onion

2 to 3 tablespoons (18 to 27 g) minced jalapeño, to taste

2 cloves garlic, minced

¾ cup (135 g) diced fire-roasted tomatoes (drained before measuring)

1 to 2 tablespoons (15 to 30 ml) adobo sauce, to taste

1 cup (164 g) frozen corn kernels, thawed and drained, optional

Salt and pepper

⅓ cup (5 g) chopped fresh cilantro leaves

YIELD: 4 servings
PROTEIN CONTENT PER SERVING: 16 g

In a large skillet, heat the oil on medium-high. Add the crumbled tofu, turmeric, cumin, and black salt. Stir once to combine. Sauté for 8 minutes, stirring only occasionally, or until browned, and scraping the bottom of the pan with a wooden spatula to get all the browned up bits.

Add the nutritional yeast and sauté for another 2 minutes. Add the onions, jalapeño, and garlic. Sauté for another 2 minutes until the veggies start to soften.

In the meantime, combine the drained tomatoes and adobo sauce in a small bowl. Add to the tofu mixture and sauté for another 2 minutes, stirring to combine. Add the corn and sauté for 2 minutes, until heated through. Adjust the seasonings if needed and serve garnished with cilantro.

Leftovers can be stored in an airtight container in the refrigerator for up to 3 days and reheated in a skillet on medium heat until heated through.

Recipe Notes

• This colorful scrambled tofu is great on its own. It's also exceptional when served inside fresh corn tortillas with avocado slices. Drizzle with lime or lemon juice and serve with some salsa fresca.

• If you want to boost your breakfast- or brunch-time protein (and fiber!) intake while keeping the fiesta theme going, you can add 1½ cups (258 g) of cooked black or pinto beans to the mix at the same time you add the corn. If you only have a modest appetite, this will increase the total servings to 6.

FOR THE SCRAMBLE:

1 to 2 tablespoons (15 to 30 ml) high-heat neutral-flavored oil

1 pound (454 g) extra-firm tofu, drained and pressed, then crumbled

½ cup (72 g) chopped bell pepper (any color)

⅓ cup (53 g) chopped red onion

2 teaspoons ground cumin

1 teaspoon ground coriander

1 teaspoon caraway seeds

½ teaspoon paprika

½ teaspoon ground allspice

½ teaspoon chili powder

2 tablespoons (15 g) nutritional yeast

10 cherry tomatoes, halved

2 teaspoons capers, drained

2 cloves garlic, minced

1¼ cups (178 g) sauerkraut, drained but not squeezed (some juice reserved)

3 tablespoons (45 ml) reserved sauerkraut juice

3 tablespoons (45 ml) vegetable broth, or water

1 tablespoon (16 g) tomato paste

¼ teaspoon liquid smoke, or to taste

Salt and pepper

FOR THE 'WICHES:

4 slices of rye bread, toasted

Dijon mustard

2 handfuls baby spinach

3 dill pickles, sliced thinly

YIELD: 4 servings
PROTEIN CONTENT PER SERVING: 16 g

Reuben Scramble 'Wiches

▶ QUICK AND EASY

Whether you choose to make these for a savory breakfast dish or a light dinner, you'll love the way the spices in the tofu mingle with the sauerkraut to create this very satisfying open-faced sandwich.

To make the scramble: Heat 1 tablespoon (15 ml) of the oil in a large skillet over medium-high heat. Add the crumbled tofu, reduce the heat to medium, and let cook until browned, stirring occasionally. Add the additional tablespoon (15 ml) of oil if the tofu is sticking. Cook until well browned, about 10 minutes. Add the bell pepper and onion, and cook until the onions soften, about 3 minutes. Add the spices, nutritional yeast, cherry tomatoes, capers, garlic, and sauerkraut. Cook for 3 to 4 minutes, stirring to combine.

Whisk together the sauerkraut juice, broth or water, tomato paste, and liquid smoke in a small bowl. Pour into the tofu and cook for 4 to 5 minutes, stirring occasionally. The liquid should be absorbed by the tofu. Season to taste with salt and pepper.

To make the 'wiches: Spread each slice of toast with a thin layer of mustard. Divide the spinach evenly on the toast, and then layer with the dill pickles. Divide the tofu mixture evenly over top and serve immediately.

20-Minute Tofu Soup

▶ QUICK AND EASY ▶ GLUTEN-FREE POTENTIAL

This quick soup only requires 10 minutes of prep and another 10 minutes of simmering. It's the perfect dish for the night you get home from work later than you thought or when you are feeling under the weather. We like to think of it as a sniffle-stopping soup.

1 tablespoon (15 ml) neutral-flavored oil

1 teaspoon toasted sesame oil

⅓ cup (53 g) minced shallot

¼ cup (40 g) minced garlic

2 teaspoons grated fresh ginger root

8 ounces (227 g) extra-firm tofu, drained, pressed, cut into very thin slices, then into ¼-inch (6 mm) pieces

½ cup plus 2 tablespoons (90 g) daikon matchsticks

3 tablespoons (43 g) minced carrot

¼ teaspoon ground white pepper

¼ teaspoon cayenne pepper, or to taste

2½ cups (590 ml) vegetable broth

3 tablespoons (45 ml) tamari

2 tablespoons (30 ml) seasoned rice vinegar

1 teaspoon sambal oelek, or to taste

Minced scallion, for garnish

YIELD: 3 to 4 servings

PROTEIN CONTENT PER SERVING: 12 g

Heat the oils in a medium-size saucepan over medium heat. Add the shallot, garlic, and ginger. Cook for 3 minutes, stirring occasionally, until fragrant.

Add the tofu, daikon, carrot, white pepper, and cayenne pepper. Some of the tofu may break, and that is okay. Cook for 2 minutes, stirring.

Add the broth, tamari, vinegar, and sambal oelek. Bring to a boil, and then reduce to a simmer. Cook for 10 minutes. Serve garnished with scallion.

Tempeh Noodle Soup

This home-style soup has a savory broth with a depth of flavor that showcases the tempeh wonderfully. We love how the texture of the protein-rich tempeh is the ideal counterpoint to the pasta.

4 ounces (113 g) capellini, angel hair, or other thin pasta

8 ounces (227 g) tempeh, simmered, and cut into small cubes

2 tablespoons (30 ml) high heat neutral-flavored oil

1 medium onion, minced (about 1½ cups, or 240 g)

2 carrots, chopped (about ¾ cup, or 98 g)

1 stalk celery, chopped (about ½ cup, or 60 g)

3 cloves garlic, minced

1 teaspoon ground cumin

1 teaspoon dried mustard

1 teaspoon onion powder

1 teaspoon dried poultry seasoning

1 teaspoon dried thyme

½ teaspoon ground white pepper

½ teaspoon turmeric

¼ cup (60 ml) dry white wine, or vegetable broth

5 to 6 cups (1.2 to 1.4 L) water

2 tablespoons (15 g) nutritional yeast

1 tablespoon (18 g) no chicken bouillon paste

¼ cup (33 g) frozen peas, thawed

1 tablespoon (4 g) fresh minced parsley

Salt and pepper

YIELD: 4 servings
PROTEIN CONTENT PER SERVING: 19 g

Bring a medium-size pot of salted water to a boil. Break the capellini into 1-inch (2.5 cm) pieces and cook al dente according to the package directions. Drain and rinse under cold water. Set aside.

Heat the oil in a large soup pot over medium-high heat. Cook the tempeh for 7 to 9 minutes, stirring occasionally, until browned. Transfer to a plate and set aside. Add the onion, carrots, and celery to the soup pot. Cook for 4 to 6 minutes, stirring occasionally. Add the garlic through the turmeric and cook another minute to lightly toast the spices. Add the wine or broth and scrape up any bits from the bottom of the pot. Return the tempeh to the pot and add 5 cups (1.2 L) of water, the nutritional yeast, and bouillon. Bring to a boil, and then reduce the heat to simmer. Add the additional cup (235 ml) of water, if desired. Cook for 20 minutes. Add the peas and cook for 2 minutes longer. Stir in the noodles and parsley. Taste and adjust the seasonings before serving.

Recipe Notes

• For Seitan Noodle Soup, omit the tempeh and substitute 8 ounces (227 g) of Quit-the-Cluck Seitan (page 138), chopped. The rest of the recipe remains the same.

• For Tempeh Miso Soup, remove 1 cup (235 ml) hot broth from the soup pot. Whisk in 1 tablespoon (18 g) dark miso. Stir into the pot with the noodles and parsley.

Jerk Tempeh Salad

▶ GLUTEN-FREE POTENTIAL

This tempeh salad has a nice heat, but certainly won't sound any alarms. If you're a spice lover, feel free to add an extra scotch bonnet and also more minced jalapeño. We like to serve this salad on a bed of baby spinach or with spinach in a wrap, similar to the chicken salad of yesteryear.

8 ounces (227 g) tempeh, simmered (see page 15)

½ cup (80 g) chopped red onion

1 scotch bonnet or habanero pepper, stem and seeds removed

3 tablespoons (45 ml) olive oil, divided

2 tablespoons (30 ml) vegetable broth

1 tablespoon (15 ml) fresh lime juice

1 tablespoon (20 g) pure maple syrup

½ inch (1.3 cm) piece fresh ginger root, peeled

3 cloves garlic

¼ teaspoon fine sea salt

Pinch of ground black pepper

Nonstick cooking spray

¼ cup plus 2 tablespoons (68 g) chopped fresh mango

¼ cup (36 g) chopped red bell pepper

3 tablespoons (18 g) chopped scallion

2 tablespoons (15 g) minced celery

1 tablespoon (9 g) minced jalapeño, or to taste

2 teaspoons minced fresh thyme

⅓ cup (75 g) vegan mayonnaise, more if needed

1 teaspoon red wine vinegar

YIELD: 3 cups (510 g), or 6 servings
PROTEIN CONTENT PER SERVING: 8 g

Cut the tempeh into ½-inch (1.3 cm) cubes.

Combine the onion, scotch bonnet, 1 tablespoon (15 ml) olive oil, and the broth through the black pepper in a small blender. Blend until smooth. Pour the marinade into a shallow container. Add the tempeh cubes and coat them with the marinade. Stir the cubes occasionally. Cover, and marinate in the refrigerator for 12 hours, or up to 2 days.

Preheat the oven to 400°F (200°C, or gas mark 6). Spray a 9 x 13 inch (22 x 33 cm) glass baking dish with cooking spray.

Pour the tempeh and marinade into the baking dish. Bake for 15 minutes, and then remove from the oven. Stir in the remaining 2 tablespoons (30 ml) olive oil and return the tempeh to the oven to bake for 30 minutes longer or until slightly crisp. Let the tempeh cool completely before continuing.

Combine the tempeh and remaining ingredients in a medium-size bowl. Stir well, cover, and refrigerate for at least 30 minutes, or up to 2 days before serving. When serving, stir in extra mayonnaise, if needed, and taste and adjust the seasonings.

Provençale Tofu Salad Sandwiches

It's no secret that we have a thing for vegan sandwiches, and this one is our newest favorite. Say hello to a festival of flavors and textures, stuck between two slices of sourdough bread!

1½ teaspoons neutral-flavored oil

1 pound (454 g) super firm tofu, cut into ¼-inch (6 mm) cubes

1½ teaspoons vegan Worcestershire sauce

½ cup (112 g) vegan mayonnaise

3 tablespoons (30 g) minced red onion

¼ cup (30 g) coarsely chopped toasted walnuts

3 tablespoons (11 g) minced fresh parsley

2 tablespoons (13 g) minced pitted kalamata olives

1 tablespoon (4 g) minced soft or oil-packed (rinsed and patted dry) sun-dried tomatoes

1 tablespoon (15 ml) white balsamic vinegar

1 tablespoon (15 ml) fresh lemon juice

2 teaspoons minced capers

1 large or 2 small cloves of garlic, grated or pressed

½ teaspoon herbes de Provence or dried basil

¼ teaspoon red pepper flakes

White or black ground pepper

Salt

12 to 18 slices of vegan sourdough bread or favorite vegan bread, toasted

Favorite vegan pesto, as needed

YIELD: 6 to 9 sandwiches, 3 cups (540 g) tofu salad

PROTEIN CONTENT PER SANDWICH (WITH SALAD): 5 g

Place the oil in a large skillet and heat on medium-high heat. Add the tofu and sauté until lightly browned, stirring often, for about 6 minutes. Add the Worcestershire sauce and stir to combine, sautéing another 2 minutes. Remove from the heat to let cool.

In a large bowl, combine the mayonnaise, onion, walnuts, parsley, olives, sun-dried tomatoes, vinegar, lemon juice, capers, garlic, herbes de Provence, red pepper flakes, and pepper. Stir the cooled tofu into the mayonnaise mixture. Adjust the seasonings if needed. Cover and place in the refrigerator for at least 3 hours, or overnight, to let the flavors blend.

Spread a thin layer of pesto on all bread slices. Place ⅓ cup (60 g) of tofu salad evenly on a slice of bread or as much as will fit on the slice. Be careful not to be too generous, so that the tofu cubes don't fall out as you eat. Cover with a second slice of bread. Repeat until you run out of ingredients. The yield will vary depending on the size of the sliced bread.

Leftovers of the salad can be stored in an airtight container in the refrigerator for up to 4 days.

Recipe Note

The advantage of super firm tofu is that it cuts down on prep time: There's no need to press it, so it's also less of a waste of paper towels if you don't have one of those fancy tofu presses. (But if you can only find extra-firm tofu, it will work here too.)

Sloppy Joe Scramble Stuffed Spuds

This is the sloppy joe filling that you *wish* your mom made. We like the potato boats, but if you prefer to use buns, go wild. Serve these as a protein-rich appetizer or alongside a salad for a meal.

1 to 2 tablespoons (15 to 30 ml) high heat neutral-flavored oil

1 pound (454 g) extra-firm tofu, drained, pressed, and crumbled

½ teaspoon fine sea salt

¼ teaspoon ground black pepper

¾ cup (120 g) minced onion

½ cup (75 g) minced bell pepper (any color)

3 cloves garlic, minced

1 tablespoon (7 g) ground cumin

2 teaspoons chili powder, or to taste

1 can (15 ounces, or 425 ml) tomato sauce

2 tablespoons (30 g) organic ketchup

1 tablespoon (15 ml) tamari

1 tablespoon (15 ml) vegan Worcestershire sauce

1 tablespoon (11 g) prepared yellow mustard

1 (4-inch or 10 cm) dill pickle, minced

¾ cup (180 ml) water (put in the emptied tomato sauce can)

3 baked potatoes, cooled

1 tablespoon (15 ml) olive oil

YIELD: 6 potato halves

PROTEIN CONTENT PER POTATO HALF: 12 g

Heat 1 tablespoon (15 ml) of oil in a large skillet over medium-high heat. If the skillet is not well-seasoned, add the remaining tablespoon (15 ml) of oil. Add the tofu, salt, and pepper. Cook for 8 to 10 minutes, stirring occasionally, until the tofu is firm and golden. Stir in the onion, bell pepper, garlic, cumin, and chili powder. Reduce the heat to medium and cook for 3 minutes, stirring occasionally, until fragrant. Add the tomato sauce, ketchup, tamari, Worcestershire sauce, mustard, and dill pickle. Bring to a boil, and then reduce the heat to simmer. Swish the water in the tomato sauce can to clean the sides. Simmer for 30 minutes, stirring occasionally, adding the water from the tomato sauce can, as needed, for the desired consistency.

Preheat the oven to broil. Cut the baked potatoes in half lengthwise. Scoop the insides from the potatoes, leaving about ½ inch (1.3 cm) of the skin intact. Brush both the insides and the outsides of the potato skins with the olive oil and place on a baking sheet. Broil for 3 to 4 minutes until lightly browned. Remove from the oven and divide the filling evenly in the potatoes, using about ¾ cup (130 g) in each.

Recipe Notes

• As tomatoes can vary in acidity, add about a teaspoon of agave nectar or sugar, if desired, to taste.

• The leftover insides of the potatoes are a terrific soup thickener.

Smoky Bean and Tempeh Patties

Combining beans with crumbled tempeh is a great way to reach protein nirvana. It also makes for patties that boast a rather meaty and fantastic texture. You can serve these in the form of classic burgers with your favorite accompaniments, or see the Recipe Note below.

1 cup (177 g) cooked cannellini beans

8 ounces (227 g) tempeh

½ cup (91 g) cooked bulgur

2 cloves garlic, pressed

1½ teaspoons onion powder

4 teaspoons (20 ml) liquid smoke

4 teaspoons (20 ml) vegan Worcestershire sauce

1 teaspoon smoked paprika

2 tablespoons (30 g) organic ketchup

2 tablespoons (40 g) pure maple syrup

2 tablespoons (30 ml) neutral-flavored oil

3 tablespoons (45 ml) tamari

½ cup (60 g) chickpea flour

Nonstick cooking spray

YIELD: 8 patties
PROTEIN CONTENT PER PATTY: 10 g

Mash the beans in a large bowl: It's okay if a few small pieces of beans are left. Crumble (do not mash) the tempeh into small pieces on top. Add the bulgur and garlic. In a medium bowl, whisk together the remaining ingredients, except the flour and cooking spray. Stir into the crumbled tempeh preparation. Add the flour and mix until well combined. Chill for 1 hour before shaping into patties.

Preheat the oven to 350°F (180°C, or gas mark 4). Line a baking sheet with parchment paper. Scoop out a packed ⅓ cup (96 g) per patty, shaping into an approximately 3-inch (8 cm) circle and flattening slightly on the prepared sheet. You should get eight 3.5-inch (9 cm) patties in all. Lightly coat the top of the patties with cooking spray. Bake for 15 minutes, carefully flip, lightly coat the top of the patties with cooking spray, and bake for another 15 minutes until lightly browned and firm.

Leftovers can be stored in an airtight container in the refrigerator for up to 4 days. The patties can also be frozen, tightly wrapped in foil, for up to 3 months.

If you don't eat all the patties at once, reheat the leftovers on low heat in a skillet lightly greased with olive oil or cooking spray for about 5 minutes on each side until heated through.

Recipe Note

We love to serve these patties with Creamy Cashew Sauce (page 92), mashed potatoes, and roasted broccoli or cauliflower for a comfort food type of meal. They can also be served as a savory breakfast item alongside any favorite tofu scramble and some toast.

Tempeh Banh Mi

Freshly pickled vegetables, a spicy sauce, and savory marinated tempeh all combine to create layers of spicy, pickley, sourish-sweet, umami wonder and one of our favorite sandwiches.

3 tablespoons (45 ml) tamari

2 tablespoons (30 ml) seasoned rice vinegar, divided

½ teaspoon onion powder

½ teaspoon garlic powder

½ teaspoon ginger powder

¼ teaspoon cayenne pepper

8 ounces (227 g) tempeh, simmered, cut in half laterally, then vertically to form 4 thin patties

½ cup (72 g) daikon matchsticks

½ cup (112 g) cucumber matchsticks

½ cup (56 g) grated carrots

2 tablespoons (10 g) minced scallion

1 tablespoon (9 g) minced jalapeño, or to taste

1 tablespoon (15 ml) fresh lime juice

½ teaspoon agave nectar, or to taste

1 clove garlic, minced

¼ teaspoon grated fresh ginger root

Salt and pepper

¼ cup (56 g) vegan mayonnaise

2 teaspoons sriracha, or to taste

High heat neutral-flavored oil, for cooking the tempeh

4 (5-inch, or 13 cm) pieces of French bread, sliced in half laterally, some insides removed, toasted

Handful fresh cilantro leaves

8 leaves romaine lettuce

YIELD: 4 sandwiches

PROTEIN CONTENT PER SANDWICH: 41 g

Combine the tamari, 1 tablespoon (15 ml) vinegar, the onion powder, garlic powder, ginger powder, and cayenne pepper in an 8 x 11 inch (20 x 28 cm) baking dish. Put the tempeh patties into the marinade. Marinate for 1 hour or cover and refrigerate up to 12 hours.

Stir together the daikon, cucumber, carrots, scallion, jalapeño, remaining tablespoon (15 ml) vinegar, lime juice, agave, garlic, and fresh ginger in a medium-size bowl. Season to taste. Cover and refrigerate for 1 hour. Longer refrigeration (up to 2 days) will lead to a more pickled flavor.

Stir together the mayonnaise and sriracha in small bowl. Cover and refrigerate.

Heat a thin layer of oil in a large skillet over medium-high heat. Cook the tempeh for 3 to 5 minutes until browned. Turn over to cook the second side for 3 to 4 minutes also until browned.

To assemble the sandwiches, spread the inside tops and bottoms of the bread evenly with the spiced mayonnaise. Place a piece of tempeh on each bottom. Using a slotted spoon, top the tempeh with one-quarter of the pickled vegetables, a few pieces of fresh cilantro (to taste), and two lettuce leaves. Put the tops on the sandwiches and serve.

Recipe Notes

• If Thai basil is available, add a couple leaves to each sandwich for yet another layer of flavor.

• If serving these to people with varied heat preferences, add sliced jalapeños to the spice lovers' sandwiches.

Italian Meatfree Balls

With their slightly crisp exterior and inner tenderness, these meatfree balls are made protein-rich thanks to the combination of blended silken tofu, vital wheat gluten (which also gives them their awesome texture), and nutritional yeast (which also lends them a slightly cheesy flavor). It's teamwork at its best!

8 ounces (227 g) blended soft silken tofu

2 tablespoons (30 ml) olive oil

2 tablespoons (30 ml) fresh lemon juice

2½ tablespoons (10 g) sun-dried tomatoes (drained and rinsed if packed in oil), minced

1 tablespoon (9 g) capers, drained and minced

¼ cup (30 g) nutritional yeast

1½ teaspoons onion powder

2 cloves garlic, pressed

Scant ½ teaspoon fine salt

1 teaspoon dried basil

½ teaspoon dried thyme

½ teaspoon dried oregano

½ cup (72 g) vital wheat gluten

1 cup (80 g) panko crumbs

Nonstick cooking spray or oil spray

Favorite vegan marinara sauce, for serving

YIELD: 16 to 18 meatfree balls
PROTEIN CONTENT PER BALL: 8 g

Preheat the oven to 350°F (180°C, or gas mark 4). Line a baking sheet with parchment paper or a silicone baking mat.

In a large bowl, stir the tofu, oil, lemon juice, sun-dried tomatoes, capers, nutritional yeast, onion powder, garlic, salt, basil, thyme, and oregano until combined.

Add the vital wheat gluten and panko crumbs on top and stir again until thoroughly combined.

Scoop 2 packed tablespoons (28 g) per ball. Shape into a ball and place on the prepared baking sheet. Repeat until you run out of the mixture: You should get 16 to 18 balls in all.

Lightly coat the top of the balls with cooking spray.

Bake for 14 minutes, flip, lightly coat the other side with cooking spray, and bake for another 8 minutes or until golden brown.

Remove from the oven and let stand a few minutes before serving with your favorite marinara.

Tempeh Tortilla Pizzas

▶ QUICK AND EASY

Minced tempeh fills in well as the "meat" in these Mexican-inspired pizzas. Adding your own favorite toppings will launch these into regular rotation in your home.

2 (10-inch, or 25 cm) flour tortillas

Nonstick cooking spray

2 teaspoons onion powder

1 teaspoon garlic powder

1 teaspoon ground cumin

1 teaspoon chili powder

1 teaspoon dried oregano

8 ounces (227 g) tempeh, simmered, finely minced

1 tablespoon (15 ml) high heat neutral-flavored oil, more if needed

2 tablespoons (30 ml) vegetable broth, more as needed

1 tablespoon (15 ml) tamari

1 chipotle in adobe, or to taste

3 cups (165 g) shredded lettuce

½ cup (90 g) chopped tomato

2 tablespoons (12 g) minced scallion

1 large or 2 small avocados, pitted and peeled

2 to 4 tablespoons (33 to 66 g) salsa, as desired

Salt and pepper

YIELD: 2 (10-inch, or 25 cm) tortilla pizzas, or 4 servings

PROTEIN CONTENT PER SERVING: 17 g

Preheat the oven to 400°F (200°C, or gas mark 6). Lightly coat the tortillas with the cooking spray. Bake for 2 to 3 minutes until golden (see Recipe Note). Turn over, spray the second side, and bake for 2 to 3 minutes until they reach the desired crispness. Longer baking will lead to a cracker-like crust.

Combine the onion powder, garlic powder, cumin, chili powder, and oregano in a medium-size bowl. Toss the minced tempeh in the seasonings to coat. Heat the oil in a large skillet over medium-high heat. Add the tempeh and cook for 3 to 5 minutes, stirring occasionally, until lightly browned. Add an additional tablespoon (15 ml) of oil if necessary to keep it from sticking.

Combine 2 tablespoons (30 ml) of the broth, tamari, and chipotle in a small blender. Process until smooth. Pour over the tempeh and cook for 3 to 5 minutes, stirring occasionally. Add additional splashes of broth to keep the mixture moist, as needed. The tempeh should absorb the liquid. Season to taste with salt and pepper.

Toss the lettuce, tomato, and scallion together.

Mash the avocado. Spread the avocado evenly on the tortillas and season with salt and pepper. Top with the tempeh mixture, spreading it evenly. Layer with the lettuce mixture. Spoon the salsa on the tortillas as desired.

Recipe Note

The thickness of tortillas varies. When baking, keep an eye on them so they are golden and crisp, but not burnt.

FOR THE SIMPLE CASHEW DIP:

¾ cup (180 g) cashew base (page 91)

1½ tablespoons (6 g) packed minced fresh parsley

1½ tablespoons (23 ml) fresh lemon juice

1½ tablespoons (24 g) tahini

1 to 2 cloves garlic, grated or pressed, to taste

Salt and pepper

FOR THE KOFTAS:

Nonstick cooking spray

1 cup (177 g) cannellini beans or 1 cup (171 g) black-eyed peas

8 ounces (227 g) tempeh

¼ cup (40 g) minced red onion

¼ cup (16 g) packed flat leaf parsley, minced

2 tablespoons (30 ml) neutral-flavored oil, plus extra for brushing

1 tablespoon (15 g) harissa paste

3 large cloves garlic, grated or pressed

1½ teaspoons ground coriander

1 teaspoon ground cumin

¾ teaspoon fine sea salt

½ teaspoon ground cinnamon

½ teaspoon ground allspice

¼ teaspoon ground nutmeg

2 tablespoons (15 g) whole wheat pastry flour or (16 g) all-purpose flour

2 tablespoons (30 ml) fresh lemon juice, optional

Olive oil, for brushing

YIELD: 20 koftas, plus 1 scant cup (230 g) dip

PROTEIN CONTENT PER KOFTA (WITH SAUCE): 6 g

Tempeh Koftas with Cashew Dip

These Middle Eastern–flavored, spicy meatballs are even more fantastic when served alongside a lightly-dressed carrot salad.

To make the koftas: Lightly coat 20 cups of a 24-cup mini muffin tin with cooking spray.

Mash the beans or peas in a large bowl: It's okay if just a few pieces of beans are left. Crumble (do not mash) the tempeh into small pieces on top. Add the onion, parsley, oil, harissa paste, garlic, coriander, cumin, salt, cinnamon, allspice, nutmeg, and flour on top.

Stir to combine. If the mixture is dry and doesn't hold together, add the lemon juice and stir to combine again. Shape 1 packed, rounded tablespoon (about 25 g) of the mixture into a ball, and place in the prepared muffin tin. Repeat with remaining koftas. Loosely cover with plastic wrap and store in the refrigerator for 1 hour.

Preheat the oven to 350°F (180°C, or gas mark 4).

Lightly brush each kofta with oil. Bake for 15 minutes, gently flip (the koftas will be fragile), and lightly brush with oil again. Bake for another 10 minutes, or until golden brown.

Let stand 10 minutes in the muffin tin to set before serving, as the koftas will be fragile right out of the oven. Serve with the cashew dip. The koftas are also delicious without the dip.

To make the dip: Combine all the ingredients in a food processor until smooth. Occasionally stop to scrape the sides with a rubber spatula. Cover and store in the refrigerator for at least 1 hour until ready to serve. Leftovers can be stored in an airtight container in the refrigerator for up to 3 days. The dip will thicken after more than 24 hours of refrigeration. Use it as is to spread on bread or thin it by adding more lemon juice to taste.

Maple Dijon Tempeh Fingers

You too are bound to be surprised by how crisp the breading of these tempeh fingers is and yet how tenderly flaky the tempeh remains inside! If you cannot find vegan saltines, you can use ¾ cup (81 g) of fine vegan bread crumbs or another crushed vegan cracker (like Late July Rich Crackers).

FOR THE TEMPEH FINGERS:

3 tablespoons (45 g) mild Dijon mustard

2 tablespoons (40 g) pure maple syrup

1 tablespoon (15 ml) olive oil

1 clove garlic, grated or pressed

2 teaspoons pure lemon juice

2 teaspoons tamari

2 teaspoons tahini or cashew butter

2 teaspoons nutritional yeast

8 ounces (227 g) tempeh, cut widthwise into ½-inch (1.3 cm) fingers

Half a sleeve of vegan saltines (about 20 crackers, or 60 g), finely crushed (See headnote.)

1 teaspoon onion powder

½ teaspoon paprika

½ teaspoon dried basil

Pinch of fine sea salt

Pinch of ground black or white pepper

Nonstick cooking spray or oil spray

FOR THE DIPPING SAUCE:

2 tablespoons (30 g) pure maple syrup

1 tablespoon (15 g) mild Dijon mustard

1 tablespoon (15 g) vegan mayonnaise or (15 g) unsweetened plain vegan yogurt

YIELD: 10 to 12 tempeh fingers, plus scant ½ cup (105 ml) dipping sauce

PROTEIN CONTENT PER TEMPEH FINGER (WITH SAUCE): 5 g

To make the tempeh fingers: In an 8-inch (20 cm) square baking dish, whisk the mustard, maple syrup, oil, garlic, lemon juice, tamari, tahini or cashew butter, and nutritional yeast to thoroughly combine. Dip the cut tempeh in the somewhat thick and sticky marinade, making sure every side of the tempeh gets coated, including the tips. Cover and store in the refrigerator for at least 2 hours, flipping once halfway through, or up to overnight. Do not discard the marinade leftovers! They will be stirred into the dipping sauce ingredients.

Preheat the oven to 375°F (190°C, or gas mark 5). Line a large baking sheet with parchment paper. (Make the dipping sauce while the tempeh fingers are in the oven.)

In a shallow bowl, combine the crushed saltines, onion powder, paprika, dried basil, salt, and pepper.

Dip each tempeh finger into the crushed saltines, gently and generously patting the crumbs on top to make sure they adhere. Transfer to the prepared sheet. Repeat with the remaining tempeh fingers. Lightly coat with cooking spray.

Bake for 10 minutes. Flip to the other side and lightly coat with cooking spray again. Bake for another 10 minutes. Remove from the oven.

To make the dipping sauce: In a small bowl, whisk the maple syrup, mustard, mayonnaise or yogurt, and remaining marinade to thoroughly combine. Serve with the tempeh fingers.

Tofu Tempura

We're just coming out with it: This isn't the healthiest recipe in the book, but there are times that just call for tempura! Ours is crisp, light, and the ultimate indulgence. We like to have green beans, onion slices, or mushrooms ready for any extra batter. As an added bonus, the vegetable tempura is the ideal accompaniment to the tofu.

FOR THE CILANTRO DIPPING SAUCE:

2 tablespoons (28 g) vegan mayonnaise

1 teaspoon minced fresh cilantro

1 teaspoon minced scallion

½ teaspoon sriracha, or to taste

FOR THE TAMARI DIPPING SAUCE:

2 tablespoons (30 ml) tamari

2 teaspoons seasoned rice vinegar

1 clove garlic, minced

¼ teaspoon grated fresh ginger root

FOR THE TEMPURA:

8 ounces (227 g) extra-firm tofu, drained and pressed, sliced into ¼-inch (6 mm) strips, lengthwise

2 tablespoons (30 ml) tamari

2 tablespoons (30 ml) seasoned rice vinegar

2 tablespoons (30 ml) dry white wine, or vegetable broth

High heat neutral-flavored oil, for cooking

½ cup (62 g) all-purpose flour

½ cup (80 g) white rice flour

½ teaspoon turmeric

¼ teaspoon cayenne pepper

¼ teaspoon fine sea salt

1 cup (235 ml) ice cold water

YIELD: About 26 pieces
PROTEIN CONTENT PER PIECE: 2 g

To make the sauces: Combine the ingredients for each sauce in separate bowls. Cover and refrigerate. If making only one sauce, double the recipe.

To make the tempura: Mix together the tamari, vinegar, and wine or broth in a 9-inch (23 cm) square baking dish. Add the tofu slices, and turn to coat. Marinate for 1 hour, or up to 24 hours, refrigerated. Heat at least 2 inches (5 cm) of oil in a large, deep, heavy-bottomed skillet or in a deep fryer, following manufacturer's directions. The temperature should be 360 to 375°F (180 to 190°C).

Stir the flours, turmeric, cayenne pepper, and salt together in a medium-size bowl. Stir in the cold water. It is alright if the batter is lumpy. It's important to not overwork the batter: It should be the consistency of pancake batter. Add additional water 1 tablespoon (15 ml) at a time or (8 g) all-purpose flour, if needed. The batter should lightly coat the tofu, with the excess dripping into the bowl. Working in batches, dip the tofu in the batter, and then carefully place in the oil. Cook for 3 to 4 minutes until golden brown. Transfer to a baking rack placed over a large rimmed baking sheet to let excess oil drip off. Continue until all the tofu is cooked. Serve immediately with the sauces.

Recipe Note

For the lightest tempura, it's important to use very cold batter and hot oil. If the oil is not hot enough, the tempura will be heavy and oily.

Tofu Fried Rice

▶ QUICK AND EASY ▶ GLUTEN-FREE POTENTIAL

We wanted a recipe that was Tofu Fried Rice, rather than Fried Rice with Tofu, because (stating the obvious) this is a protein book. The rice is here for support, but some of our testers thought it could use another cup (158 g). Either way, you'll end up with a cooked-in-your-own-way main dish or side.

1 pound (454 g) extra-firm tofu, drained and pressed

2 tablespoons (30 ml) high heat neutral-flavored oil, divided

1 teaspoon toasted sesame oil

¼ cup (60 ml) tamari, divided, or to taste

1 cup (75 g) sugar snap peas, trimmed

¾ cup (120 g) chopped onion

¾ cup (75 g) chopped scallion, divided

¼ cup (38 g) chopped bell pepper (any color)

1 cup (70 g) chopped mushrooms (any kind)

2 cups (390 g) cooked, cooled basmati rice (See headnote.)

2 tablespoons (30 ml) seasoned rice vinegar

2 teaspoons sriracha, or to taste

4 cloves garlic, minced

1 teaspoon grated fresh ginger root

1½ cups (156 g) bean sprouts

1 heaping cup (70 g) sliced bok choy

Salt and pepper

YIELD: 4 servings
PROTEIN CONTENT PER SERVING: 19 g

Cut the tofu into ¼-inch (6 mm) slices. Then cut each slice into thirds. Cut across each third to create 2 triangles.

Heat 1 tablespoon (15 ml) of oil in a wok or large skillet over medium-high heat. Add the tofu and cook for 5 to 7 minutes, stirring occasionally, until golden. Add 1 tablespoon (15 ml) tamari. Cook and stir until the tamari is evaporated or absorbed. Remove the tofu from the wok and set aside.

Add the remaining tablespoon (15 ml) of oil and the sesame oil to the wok. Stir in the sugar snap peas, onion, ½ cup (40 g) scallion, and bell pepper. Cook and stir for 2 to 3 minutes. The vegetables should remain crisp, but slightly brighten in color. Add the mushrooms and rice. Lower the heat to medium and stir to combine. Cook until the rice begins to crisp. This may take 10 to 15 minutes. Keep an eye on it, but don't overstir the rice or it will slow the crisping. Once the sauce is added, it will not get any more fried.

Stir together the remaining 3 tablespoons (45 ml) tamari, rice vinegar, sriracha, garlic, and ginger. Add the tamari mixture, bean sprouts, bok choy, and reserved tofu to the wok. Cook for 3 to 5 minutes, stirring occasionally until well combined. Add the salt and pepper to taste, and additional tamari, if desired. Serve topped with the remaining ¼ cup (20 g) scallion.

Best Baked Tofu

▶ GLUTEN-FREE POTENTIAL

This savory tofu can be used in a variety of ways: as is, served with gravy, as cutlets in a sandwich, or chopped and made into a no-chicken salad, to name a few. To really feature the tofu, try it in the Best Baked Tofu with Kale (page 129).

Nonstick cooking spray

1 pound (454 g) extra-firm tofu, drained, pressed, and cut into ¼-inch (6 mm) thick slices, then cut on the diagonal to form two triangles

½ cup (120 ml) vegetable broth

¼ cup (60 ml) dry white wine, or additional broth

2 tablespoons (15 g) nutritional yeast

1 tablespoon (15 ml) olive oil

2 cloves garlic, minced

1 teaspoon dried poultry seasoning

1 teaspoon no chicken bouillon paste (See Recipe Notes.)

½ teaspoon onion powder

½ teaspoon fine sea salt

¼ teaspoon garlic powder

Pinch ground white pepper

YIELD: 1 pound (454 g) tofu, or 4 servings
PROTEIN CONTENT PER SERVING: 14 g

Spray a 9 x 13 inch (23 x 33 cm) glass baking dish with cooking spray. Stir together the broth through the white pepper in the baking dish. Add the tofu and turn to coat. Marinate for 1 hour.

Preheat the oven to 400°F (200°C, or gas mark 6). Bake the tofu in the marinade for 20 minutes. Turn the tofu over, and bake for 15 to 20 minutes longer or until golden. The tofu may be baked longer for a firmer consistency, if desired.

Recipe Notes

• The no chicken bouillon paste (see page 16) can be difficult to find. If so, use 2 teaspoons dried poultry seasoning and 1 teaspoon salt instead.

• If you'd like to make your own poultry seasoning, try this: Combine 1 tablespoon (8 g) nutritional yeast, 2 teaspoons dried thyme, 1 teaspoon onion powder, ½ teaspoon dried sage, ½ teaspoon dried rosemary, ½ teaspoon dried marjoram, ½ teaspoon salt, and ½ teaspoon white pepper in a small blender. Process until powdered, and you'll have a generous 2 tablespoons (16 g) seasoning.

Best Baked Tofu and Kale

▶ QUICK AND EASY

Kale, the wonder green, is beautifully seasoned and lightly sauced, making it the perfect jumping board for our tofu "chicken." This dinner comes together quickly and tastes like more than the sum of its parts. It's quick, easy, and even company-worthy.

¼ cup (30 g) whole wheat pastry flour or (31 g) all-purpose flour

½ teaspoon ground white pepper

1 recipe Best Baked Tofu (page 128), prepared

2 tablespoons (30 ml) high heat neutral-flavored oil

3 cloves garlic, thinly sliced

¼ cup (40 g) minced shallot

2 tablespoons (7 g) minced sun-dried tomatoes (moist vacuum-packed)

4 cups (268 g) kale, chopped

1 can (14.5 ounces, or 411 g) diced tomatoes, undrained

½ cup (120 ml) vegetable broth

¼ cup (60 ml) dry white wine, or additional broth

2 tablespoons (5 g) chopped fresh basil

Juice from ½ lemon

Salt and pepper

YIELD: 4 servings

PROTEIN CONTENT PER SERVING: 19 g

Preheat the oven to 350°F (180°C, or gas mark 4). Combine the flour and pepper on a plate. Coat the baked tofu slices with the mixture.

Heat the oil in a large skillet over medium-high heat. Cook the tofu slices (in batches) for 3 to 4 minutes until browned. Turn over to cook the second side for 3 to 4 minutes until also browned. Put the tofu in the oven to keep warm.

In the same skillet, cook the garlic, shallot, and a pinch of salt over medium heat for 3 to 4 minutes, until fragrant. Add the sun-dried tomatoes, kale, tomatoes, broth, and wine (if using). Bring to a simmer, and then cook for 12 to 15 minutes until the kale is tender. Stir in the basil and lemon juice and season to taste with salt and pepper. Serve the tofu slices on top of the greens.

Recipe Note

We like to serve this over a grain. If you are eating it without, reduce the broth to ¼ cup (60 ml).

Well-Dressed Tofu Bowls

We can't get enough of the peanut butter dressing that coats these bowls! Feel free to switch things up by using another grain instead of the Sushi Rice or other vegetables you fancy more than Brussels sprouts. (Just don't forget to drizzle the dressing on top!)

FOR THE DRESSING:

¼ cup (64 g) natural creamy peanut butter

1½ tablespoons (23 ml) seasoned rice vinegar

1½ tablespoons (23 ml) fresh lemon juice

3 tablespoons (45 ml) water or vegetable broth, more if needed

1 tablespoon (15 ml) tamari

1 tablespoon (15 ml) toasted sesame oil

1 tablespoon (18 g) white miso

1½ teaspoons agave nectar or brown rice syrup

1 clove garlic, grated or pressed

FOR THE BOWLS:

1 tablespoon (15 ml) peanut oil or coconut oil

1 pound (454 g) super firm tofu, cut into ¼-inch (6 mm) cubes

10 ounces (283 g) shaved Brussels sprouts or 12 ounces (340 g) broccoli florets

½ cup (120 ml) vegetable broth, as needed

1 recipe Sushi Rice (page 28)

Sriracha, to taste

Chopped scallion

Chopped fresh cilantro

YIELD: 4 servings, plus ¾ cup (180 ml) dressing

PROTEIN CONTENT PER SERVING (WITH DRESSING): 19 g

To make the dressing: Combine all the ingredients in a small blender or if using an immersion blender in a medium glass measuring cup. Blend until perfectly smooth. If there are leftovers, you can store them in a squeeze bottle in the refrigerator for up to one week. If the dressing thickens, thin it out with either water or broth, as needed. Stir well before use.

To make the bowls: Place the oil in a large skillet. Heat on medium-high, carefully add the tofu, and sauté for about 8 minutes until the tofu cubes are golden brown on every side, stirring occasionally to keep the cubes from sticking to the skillet.

Transfer the tofu to a medium bowl. Sauté the Brussels sprouts for a couple of minutes on medium-high heat just to get them lightly browned. Add ¼ cup (60 ml) of broth, stirring to combine. Add a lid to the skillet and cook for 4 to 10 minutes (will depend on if using shaved Brussels sprouts or broccoli florets) until the vegetables are tender and the broth has evaporated. Check occasionally that the vegetables aren't attaching to the skillet. Add the remaining ¼ cup (60 ml) broth if the vegetables aren't tender enough yet and cook until tender. Remove from the heat.

To assemble the bowls: Place ¼ of the Sushi Rice at the bottom of a serving bowl. Add ¼ of the Brussels sprouts on top and ¼ of the tofu cubes. Drizzle some dressing on top. Add a few drops of sriracha, if desired, and chopped scallion and cilantro. Serve immediately.

Caribbean Tofu

▶ GLUTEN-FREE POTENTIAL

When we're looking to switch up our usual baked tofu, we like to try this twist. It can be served as cutlets, in sandwiches, on salads, or cubed, as explained in the Recipe Note.

2 teaspoons onion powder

2 teaspoons curry powder (mild or hot)

½ teaspoon ground allspice

¼ teaspoon ground nutmeg

½ teaspoon cayenne pepper

½ teaspoon turmeric

¼ cup plus 2 tablespoons (90 ml) vegetable broth

3 tablespoons (45 ml) dry white wine

2 tablespoons (30 ml) olive oil

1 teaspoon pure maple syrup

1 teaspoon liquid smoke

2 cloves garlic, minced

1 teaspoon grated fresh ginger root

½ teaspoon fine sea salt

¼ teaspoon ground white pepper

1 pound (454 g) extra-firm tofu, drained and pressed, cut into ½-inch (1.3 cm) slices

YIELD: 1 pound (454 g) tofu, or 4 servings

PROTEIN CONTENT PER SERVING: 8 g

Heat a small skillet over medium-low heat. Add the onion powder through the turmeric. Cook for 3 to 4 minutes, stirring occasionally, until slightly toasted and fragrant. Combine the toasted spices and all remaining ingredients except the tofu, in a 9 x 13 inch (23 x 33 cm) baking dish. Add the tofu and turn to coat. Marinate for 1 hour or up to 12 hours, covered and refrigerated.

Preheat the oven to 400°F (200°C, or gas mark 6). Bake the tofu for 20 minutes. Turn over and bake for 15 to 20 minutes longer to the desired tenderness.

Recipe Note

This tofu is also fantastic made into cubes, as we do for the Caribbean Tofu and Pasta (page 133). Cut the pressed tofu into 1-inch (2.5 cm) cubes. Marinate as above. Bake for 30 to 35 minutes, stirring once halfway through. If using for the pasta dish, the tofu can be baked 3 days ahead of time, and refrigerated in an airtight container until needed.

Caribbean Tofu and Pasta

▶ QUICK AND EASY

Tami and her husband, Jim, love the town of Asheville, North Carolina. One of the reasons is that the town is wonderfully vegan-friendly. This is Tami's re-creation of a signature dish from the Asheville favorite, Nine Mile Restaurant.

2 tablespoons (30 ml) olive oil

1 pound (454 g) Caribbean Tofu (page 132), prepared and baked as cubes

¾ cup (120 g) chopped red onion

½ of a bell pepper (any color), cut in strips

1 cup (70 g) sliced mushrooms (any kind)

¾ cup (90 g) ½-inch (1.3 cm) zucchini pieces

1 jalapeño pepper, minced, or to taste

2 teaspoons minced garlic

1 teaspoon grated fresh ginger root

1 tablespoon (6 g) curry powder

2 teaspoons dried thyme

½ teaspoon ground allspice

¼ teaspoon cayenne pepper, or to taste

¼ teaspoon ground nutmeg

½ teaspoon fine sea salt

¼ teaspoon ground white pepper

¼ cup (60 ml) dry white wine

1 can (15 ounces, or 425 g) diced fire-roasted tomatoes, undrained

1 can (15 ounces, or 425 g) crushed fire-roasted tomatoes, undrained

12 ounces (340 g) linguini, cooked and drained

Sliced scallion, for garnish

Lime wedges, for garnish

Heat the oil in a large skillet over medium-high heat. Cook the tofu cubes for 7 to 9 minutes, stirring occasionally, until crisp. Remove the tofu from the skillet and set aside.

To the same skillet, add the onion and bell pepper. Reduce the heat to medium and cook and stir for 3 minutes, or until fragrant. Add the mushrooms, zucchini, and jalapeño. Cook, stirring, for 3 to 5 minutes, until the zucchini loses its brightness. Add the garlic, ginger, curry powder, thyme, allspice, cayenne pepper, nutmeg, salt, and pepper. Cook and stir for 3 minutes to toast the spices, but do not burn the garlic and ginger. Add the wine, scraping any bits from the bottom. Add the tomatoes and bring to a boil. Then reduce the heat to simmer for 10 minutes. Taste and adjust the seasonings.

Stir the pasta and tofu into the sauce to combine. Serve garnished with scallion and lime wedges. Diners should squeeze the lime wedges over the dish before eating.

YIELD: 4 to 6 servings

PROTEIN CONTENT PER SERVING: 18 g

Tempeh Curry

▶ GLUTEN-FREE POTENTIAL

With its firm texture and absorbent nature, tempeh tastes incredible when combined with cauliflower and earthy Indian flavors. In keeping with tradition, serve this with roti or rice—or both!

1¾ cups plus 2 tablespoons (445 ml) vegetable broth, divided

3 teaspoons ground cumin, divided

8 ounces (227 g) tempeh, simmered, cut into ¾-inch (2 cm) cubes

2 teaspoons ground coriander

2 tablespoons plus 1 teaspoon (35 ml) neutral-flavored oil, divided

½ medium red onion, minced

1 tablespoon (6 g) minced garlic

1 teaspoon grated fresh ginger root

½ teaspoon fine sea salt

1 tablespoon (6 g) curry powder (mild or hot)

½ teaspoon turmeric

½ teaspoon cayenne pepper, optional

1½ cups (150 g) cauliflower florets

½ cup (49 g) 1-inch (2.5 cm) pieces green beans

¼ cup (33 g) sliced carrot rounds

¼ cup (36 g) diced red bell pepper

3 tablespoons (48 g) tomato paste

Chopped tomato, for garnish

Minced fresh cilantro, for garnish

YIELD: 4 servings
PROTEIN CONTENT PER SERVING: 18 g

Stir together 2 tablespoons (30 ml) of broth, 2 teaspoons cumin, the coriander, and 1 teaspoon oil in an 8 x 11 inch (20 x 28 cm) baking dish. Add the tempeh cubes, stirring to coat. Marinate for 1 hour or cover and refrigerate for up to 12 hours.

Heat the remaining 2 tablespoons (30 ml) of oil in a large skillet over medium-high heat. Add the tempeh and cook for 8 to 10 minutes, stirring occasionally, until browned. Remove the tempeh and set aside. To the same skillet, add the onion and reduce the heat to medium. Cook for 3 to 5 minutes, stirring occasionally, until softened. Add the garlic, ginger, and salt and cook and stir for 2 minutes or until fragrant. Add the curry powder, turmeric, the remaining teaspoon cumin, and the cayenne pepper if desired. Cook and stir for 2 minutes. Add the cauliflower, green beans, carrots, and bell pepper, the remaining 1¾ cups (415 ml) broth, and tomato paste. Bring to a boil, and then reduce the heat to a simmer. Cook for 25 to 30 minutes, stirring occasionally, until the vegetables are the desired tenderness. Add the tempeh back to the skillet and stir to combine. Simmer for 5 minutes. Taste and adjust the seasonings. Garnish with tomato and cilantro.

Blackened Mexican Tofu, Greens, and Hash Browns

▶ QUICK AND EASY ▶ GLUTEN-FREE POTENTIAL

We love scrambles as much as the next vegan, but sometimes we like to get our breakfast protein in a really zesty way. When partnering tofu with greens and hash browns, this hearty breakfast can also stand in for a fantastic dinner.

2 teaspoons onion powder

2 teaspoons chipotle chili powder (or chili powder of choice)

1 teaspoon garlic powder

1 teaspoon smoked paprika

1 teaspoon dried oregano, crushed to a powder using fingers

½ teaspoon fine sea salt

1 pound (454 g) extra-firm tofu, drained, pressed, and cut into ½-inch (1.3 cm) slices

1 tablespoon (15 ml) high heat neutral-flavored oil

2 bunches (1½ pounds, or 681 g) Swiss chard, chopped

2 tablespoons (15 g) nutritional yeast

1 package (1 pound, or 454 g) hash browns, prepared according to package directions

1 avocado, pitted, peeled, and sliced

Salsa, for serving

YIELD: 4 servings
PROTEIN CONTENT PER SERVING: 18 g

Preheat the oven to 300°F (150°C, or gas mark 2).

Combine the onion powder, chili powder, garlic powder, smoked paprika, oregano, and salt on a plate. Coat the tofu with the spice mixture. Heat the oil in a large skillet over high heat. Test the heat of the oil by dipping a corner of tofu into it. It should sizzle. Cook the tofu slices for 3 to 5 minutes until blackened. Turn over to cook the second side for 3 to 4 minutes until also blackened. Keep warm in the oven.

Reduce the heat to medium. Put the Swiss chard into the same skillet. If the Swiss chard is freshly washed, it will still be slightly wet. If not, add a tablespoon (15 ml) of water, if needed, so it doesn't stick. Add the nutritional yeast and cook for 4 to 6 minutes, stirring occasionally, until wilted.

To serve, place one-quarter of the Swiss chard on each plate. Top with one-quarter of the hash browns and 2 to 3 pieces of tofu, depending on how many slices you were able to get. Place a few slices of avocado on the plate and serve the salsa on the side.

Recipe Note

If you prefer your breakfast on the go, after the tofu is cooked, chop it into cubes. Warm four (8-inch, or 20 cm) tortillas according to package directions. Fill the tortillas with the tofu, greens, potatoes, avocado, and salsa. Roll and wrap tightly in foil.

5

SUPER SEITAN

Welcome to the Wonders of Wheat Meat

Sometimes vegans (or vegan-curious) people miss the chewiness of animal products. With its "meaty" texture, seitan is a protein you can really bite into. Sure, portobello mushrooms are great, but seitan is in a class all its own. It can be used in a wide array of dishes—from sandwich fillings, to burritos, to pasta dishes and everything in between. We think you'll find that this is the only "meat" you'll ever need!

Kind-to-Cows Seitan

Our seitan recipes have loads of protein—and they taste amazing! We keep cutlets in the freezer, so we can thaw, and grill (or panfry) them for a quick dinner. Yes, really, they have enough flavor to serve without a sauce. But they are also sensational used in any recipe, too.

FOR THE SEITAN:

1¼ cups (180 g) vital wheat gluten

3 tablespoons (23 g) chickpea flour

1 tablespoon (10 g) granulated tapioca, such as Let's Do . . . Organic

1 tablespoon (7 g) onion powder

1 teaspoon garlic powder

½ teaspoon ground black pepper

¾ cup (180 ml) vegetable broth, more if needed

1 tablespoon (15 g) organic ketchup

2 teaspoons vegetable bouillon paste

1 tablespoon (15 ml) high heat neutral-flavored oil, for cooking

FOR THE COOKING BROTH:

2 cups (470 ml) vegetable broth

1 tablespoon (15 g) organic ketchup

1 tablespoon (15 ml) tamari

1 teaspoon liquid smoke

¼ teaspoon ground black pepper

1 teaspoon toasted sesame oil

YIELD: 6 cutlets (4 ounces, or 113 g each)
PROTEIN CONTENT PER CUTLET: 41 g

Quit-the-Cluck Seitan

▶ SOY-FREE POTENTIAL

This seitan is just as versatile as our Kind-to-Cows Seitan, but with a light, slightly herby flavor profile. Keep these in the freezer, too, for fast and easy meals. This potentially soy-free seitan can be substituted for the Kind-to-Cows Seitan in any of our recipes.

FOR THE SEITAN:

1¼ cups (150 g) vital wheat gluten

¼ cup (30 g) chickpea flour

3 tablespoons (22 g) nutritional yeast

1 tablespoon (7 g) onion powder

2 teaspoons dried poultry seasoning

1 teaspoon garlic powder

½ teaspoon ground white pepper

¾ cup (180 ml) vegetable broth, more if needed

2 teaspoons no chicken bouillon paste, or 2 cubes no chicken bouillon, crumbled

1 tablespoon (15 ml) olive oil

1 tablespoon high heat neutral-flavored oil, for cooking

FOR THE COOKING BROTH:

2 cups (470 ml) vegetable broth

1 tablespoon (8 g) nutritional yeast

2 teaspoons dried poultry seasoning

2 teaspoons onion powder

1 teaspoon Dijon mustard

Salt and pepper

YIELD: 6 cutlets (4 ounces, or 113 g each)
PROTEIN CONTENT PER CUTLET: 41 g

To make either seitan: Preheat the oven to 300°F (150°C, or gas mark 2).

Stir the dry ingredients together in a medium-size bowl. Stir the wet ingredients together in a measuring cup. Pour the wet ingredients into the dry ingredients and stir to combine. Knead with your hands until it forms a cohesive ball. Add an additional tablespoon vital wheat gluten (9 g) or broth (15 ml), if needed, to reach the desired consistency. Divide into 6 equal portions. Sandwich a portion of dough between two pieces of parchment paper. Roll each portion into a cutlet that is no more than ½-inch (1.3 cm) thick. Heat the oil in a large skillet over medium-high heat. Cook the cutlets (in batches) for 3 to 5 minutes until browned. Turn over and cook the second side for 3 minutes until browned.

To prepare either cooking broth: Stir all the ingredients together in a 9 x 13 inch (22 x 23 cm) baking dish. Put the cutlets in the broth and cover the pan tightly with foil. Bake for 1 hour. Turn off the oven and let the seitan sit in the oven for 1 hour. Cool the seitan in the broth. Store the seitan and the broth separately in airtight containers in the refrigerator for up to 3 days or freeze for up to two months.

Recipe Notes

• If the seitan is shrinking during the rolling, put it on a Silpat to help it retain its shape and size. Let it rest and reroll, as needed.

• For best texture, seitan should be refrigerated (or frozen) before using.

• If any broth is leftover, it can be frozen and used in the next batch of seitan.

• Make this into medallions or nuggets instead! Using 2 teaspoons (15 g) of dough, form into a round patty between your palms. It should be less than ¼-inch (6 mm) thick and about 1½ to 2 inches (3.8 to 5 cm) across. Panfry in batches, and then bake as above. You may need an additional tablespoon (15 ml) of oil for cooking. It will make 30 medallions (23 g each).

• To make braciola (or large cutlets to stuff and roll): Divide the dough into 4 even pieces. Roll out each piece to a 6 x 8 inch (15 x 20 cm) rectangle using the method above. Panfry in batches, and then bake as above, but in a large roasting pan using 3 cups (705 ml) of broth instead of 2 cups (470 ml). The rest of the cooking broth ingredients and directions remain the same. It will make 4 braciola-style cutlets (170 g each).

Smoky Sausages

We can't help but love anything (vegan) that contains liquid smoke, and these sausages are no exception. They're great for use in our Jumbo Pot O'Gumbo (page 157), High Brow Hash (page 100), and Veggie Sausage Frittata (page 99), but we also think they're swell to enjoy by the slice or in sandwiches too. (It's pictured here, at left, with our Put More Protein in Your Sausages, at right. See page 142.)

1¼ cups (180 g) vital wheat gluten

¼ cup (30 g) chickpea flour

¼ cup (30 g) nutritional yeast

1 tablespoon (8 g) tapioca flour

1 tablespoon (7 g) onion powder

2 teaspoons smoked paprika

1½ teaspoons ground cumin

1 teaspoon ground coriander

½ teaspoon fine sea salt (if your broth isn't very salty)

¼ teaspoon cayenne pepper

⅔ cup (160 ml) vegetable broth

2 tablespoons (30 ml) tamari

2 tablespoons (30 ml) vegan Worcestershire sauce

1 tablespoon (15 ml) neutral-flavored oil

1 tablespoon (15 ml) toasted sesame oil

1 tablespoon (16 g) tomato paste

1 to 2 tablespoons (15 to 30 ml) liquid smoke, to taste

2 teaspoons pure maple syrup

4 cloves garlic, grated or pressed

YIELD: Two 6-inch (15 cm) sausages
PROTEIN CONTENT PER SAUSAGE: 75 g

In a medium-size bowl, combine the vital wheat gluten, chickpea flour, nutritional yeast, tapioca flour, onion powder, paprika, cumin, coriander, salt, and cayenne pepper.

In a glass measuring cup, whisk to combine the broth, tamari, Worcestershire sauce, oils, tomato paste, liquid smoke, maple syrup, and garlic. Pour the liquid ingredients on top of the dry ingredients. Mix with a fork to begin with, and then use your hand directly to knead well, squeezing to be sure all ingredients are thoroughly combined.

Add an extra 1 tablespoon (15 ml) broth or (9 g) gluten if needed to make a soft, workable dough.

Divide the mixture evenly (10 ounces, or 280 g each) between two 12-inch (30 cm) pieces of foil. Form into 2 rolls of about 6 inches (15 cm) long. Roll the foil tightly around the mixture, twisting the ends to enclose the sausages.

Prepare a steamer. Steam the rolls for 1 hour 15 minutes. Remove foil (careful of the steam!) and let cool on a wire rack.

Let cool completely before slicing thinly using a sharp, serrated knife and cutting in a seesaw motion. Wrap tightly in plastic and store in the fridge for up to 1 week or freeze for up to 2 months.

Put More Protein In Your Sausages

Most gluten-based sausages are already full of protein, but what happens when you add cooked quinoa, black bean flour, nutritional yeast, and even peanut butter to the mix? Nothing but greatness, that's what. Try this sausage (pictured on page 141, on right) in our Wild Rice Pilaf with Spicy Cashews (page 86), or sliced on its own, or in Asian-style sandwiches.

1¼ cups (150 g) vital wheat gluten

¾ cup (139 g) packed cooked quinoa

¼ cup (30 g) black bean flour or chickpea flour

¼ cup (30 g) nutritional yeast

1 tablespoon (8 g) tapioca flour

1½ tablespoons (11 g) onion powder

¾ cup (180 ml) vegetable broth

¼ cup plus 1 tablespoon (80 g) natural peanut butter (crunchy or creamy)

2 tablespoons (30 ml) seasoned rice vinegar

2 tablespoons (30 ml) tamari

2 tablespoons (30 ml) sriracha

6 cloves garlic, grated or pressed

1 tablespoon (18 g) mugi miso or other flavor-packed miso

1 tablespoon (15 ml) toasted sesame oil

YIELD: Two 8-inch (20 cm) sausages
PROTEIN CONTENT PER SAUSAGE: 86 g

In a medium-size bowl, combine the vital wheat gluten, quinoa, black bean flour, nutritional yeast, tapioca flour, and onion powder.

Whisk together (or use a blender to combine) the broth, peanut butter, vinegar, tamari, sriracha, garlic, miso, and oil until thoroughly combined. Pour the liquid ingredients on top of the dry ingredients. Mix with a fork to begin with, and then use your hand directly to knead well, squeezing to be sure all ingredients are thoroughly combined.

Add an extra 1 tablespoon (15 ml) broth or (9 g) vital wheat gluten if needed to make a soft, workable dough.

Divide the mixture evenly (about 13 ounces, or 380 g each) between two 12-inch (30 cm) pieces of foil. Form into 2 rolls of about 8 inches (20 cm) long. Roll the foil tightly around the mixture, twisting the ends to enclose the sausages.

Prepare a steamer. Steam the rolls for 1 hour 15 minutes. Remove foil (careful of the steam!) and let cool on a wire rack.

Let cool completely before slicing thinly using a sharp, serrated knife and cutting in a seesaw motion. Wrap tightly in plastic and store in the fridge for up to 1 week or freeze for up to 2 months.

Sesame Seitan Super Salad

Picture this: A colorful, Asian-inspired, crisp, fresh salad featuring the amazing grain, freekeh. Now top it with a crunchy-coated, slightly spicy seitan cutlet. Are you hungry yet?

FOR THE SALAD:

⅓ cup (53 g) chopped red onion

¼ cup (60 ml) seasoned rice vinegar

1 tablespoon (12 g) sugar

1 tablespoon (15 ml) tamari

1 teaspoon Dijon mustard

1 teaspoon ginger powder

1 clove garlic, minced

3 tablespoons (45 ml) olive oil

1 package (12 ounces, or 340 g) broccoli slaw

½ cup (45 g) ½-inch (1.3 cm) pieces snow peas

⅔ cup (90 g) chopped cucumber

2 cups (150 g) napa cabbage, chopped

¾ cup (116 g) diced pineapple

2 cups (285 g) prepared whole freekeh, cooled

3 tablespoons (21 g) toasted sesame seeds

Salt and pepper

FOR THE SEITAN:

2 tablespoons (30 g) Dijon mustard

2 teaspoons sriracha

3 tablespoons (24 g) toasted sesame seeds

4 (each 4 ounces or 113 g) Quit-the-Cluck Seitan cutlets (page 138)

High heat neutral-flavored oil, for cooking

YIELD: 4 servings, plus ⅓ cup (80 ml) salad dressing

PROTEIN CONTENT PER SERVING (WITH DRESSING): 55 g

To make the salad: Start with the dressing. Combine the onion, vinegar, sugar, tamari, mustard, ginger powder, and garlic in a small blender. Process until smooth. Add the olive oil and process again.

Combine the broccoli slaw through the sesame seeds in a large bowl. Pour in the dressing, stirring to coat. Season to taste with salt and pepper and set aside.

To make the seitan: Stir together the mustard and sriracha on a plate. Spread the sesame seeds on a second plate. Dip each cutlet into the mustard mixture, then into the sesame seeds. Repeat to cover one side of all the cutlets. Pat any remaining seeds onto the cutlets.

Pour a thin layer of oil in a large skillet and heat over medium-high heat. Working in batches, sear the side without seeds for 2 to 3 minutes. Turn over to sear the seeded-side of the cutlets for 2 to 3 minutes. The sesame seeds should brown, but not burn. If moved too soon, some of the seeds will fall off. Pat them back onto the cutlets when serving.

Divide the salad evenly on four plates. Slice each cutlet into thin strips and fan a cutlet on top of each salad serving.

Quit-the-Cluck Nuggets with Mustard Chive Sauce

You probably guessed it—these were inspired by the typical fast food nuggets. That's as far as the similarity goes! Our healthy version makes a wonderful light meal or snack. They are full of protein, terrific tasting, and compassionate, too.

FOR THE NUGGETS:

½ cup (120 ml) unsweetened plain vegan milk

1 tablespoon (8 g) cornstarch

¾ cup (94 g) all-purpose flour

1½ teaspoons dried parsley

1½ teaspoons onion powder

1 teaspoon garlic powder

¼ teaspoon fine sea salt, plus a pinch

¼ teaspoon ground white pepper, plus a pinch

10 Quit-the-Cluck Seitan nuggets (page 138)

High heat neutral-flavored oil, for cooking

FOR THE SAUCE:

¼ cup (56 g) vegan mayonnaise

1 tablespoon (3 g) minced fresh chives

2 teaspoons Dijon mustard

1 teaspoon white wine vinegar

Salt and pepper

YIELD: 10 nuggets, plus ⅓ cup (57 g) sauce

PROTEIN CONTENT PER NUGGET (WITH SAUCE): 4 g

To make the nuggets: Whisk together the milk, cornstarch, and a pinch each of salt and pepper in a shallow bowl. Combine the flour, parsley, onion powder, garlic powder, ¼ teaspoon salt, and ¼ teaspoon white pepper on a plate. Line a baking sheet with parchment paper. Using one "wet" hand and one "dry" hand, dip each nugget in the milk mixture, then in the flour mixture, coating it well. Place on the lined baking sheet and continue with the remaining nuggets. Refrigerate for 30 minutes or up to 8 hours.

To make the sauce: Whisk the mayonnaise, chives, mustard, and vinegar in a small bowl. Season to taste with salt and pepper. The sauce can be made up to 24 hours in advance, covered, and refrigerated.

Preheat the oven to 300°F (150°C, or gas mark 2). Pour a thin layer of oil in a large, heavy-bottomed skillet. Heat over high heat. Cook the nuggets (in batches) for 4 to 6 minutes until golden. Reduce the heat to medium-high if the nuggets are browning too much. Turn over to cook the second side for 4 to 6 minutes until also golden. Keep warm in the oven while cooking the remaining nuggets in the same way. Serve hot with the dipping sauce.

Recipe Note

For super crispy nuggets, reduce the flour mixture by one-half. For the second dipping, use ½ cup (40 g) panko crumbs seasoned with salt and pepper.

Unicorn Tacos

▶ QUICK AND EASY

To the best of our knowledge, these are a Cleveland thing that originated at Deagan's in Lakewood, Ohio. Sweet (or not so sweet, as you prefer) chili-garlic sauce tops a crisp slaw and grilled seitan strips. For a sweeter sauce, add an additional tablespoon (12 g) sugar. Save any extra sauce in a covered container in the refrigerator for up to 1 week.

FOR THE SAUCE:

3 tablespoons (36 g) sugar

3 tablespoons (45 ml) seasoned rice vinegar

2 cloves garlic, minced

½ teaspoon onion powder

½ teaspoon fine sea salt

1 tablespoon (15 g) sambal oelek, or to taste

3 tablespoons (45 ml) cold water, more if needed

1 tablespoon (8 g) cornstarch

FOR THE TACOS:

3 cups (210 g) shredded cabbage

3 tablespoons (21 g) grated carrot

2 tablespoons (12 g) minced scallion

3 tablespoons (42 g) vegan mayonnaise

½ teaspoon Dijon mustard

8 ounces (227 g) Kind-to-Cows Seitan (page 138)

Salt and pepper

Nonstick cooking spray

4 (8-inch, or 20 cm) soft flour tortillas

YIELD: 4 tacos, plus ⅔ cup sauce (240 g)

PROTEIN CONTENT PER TACO (WITH SAUCE): 28 g

To make the sauce: Whisk the sugar, vinegar, garlic, onion powder, salt, and sambal oelek in a small saucepan over medium heat. Cook for 3 to 4 minutes until the sugar is dissolved and the mixture comes to a boil. Whisk the water and cornstarch together in a small bowl, and then pour into the sauce. Cook and whisk for 2 to 3 minutes, until thickened. Add additional water 1 tablespoon (15 ml) at a time, if needed, to get a drizzle consistency. Set aside.

To make the tacos: Toss together the cabbage, carrot, and scallion in a medium-size bowl. Stir in the mayonnaise and mustard. Season to taste with salt and pepper.

Heat a grill pan over medium-high heat. Season the cutlets with salt and pepper. Lightly coat the grill pan with the cooking spray. Grill the cutlets for 4 to 6 minutes, until they have marks. Turn over to grill the second side for 3 to 5 minutes, until they also have grill marks. Cut into thin strips.

Heat a skillet over medium-high heat. Cook the tortillas one at a time, for 1 to 2 minutes, turning them over with tongs until softened and hot.

To serve, put one-quarter of the seitan strips in each tortilla. Top with one-quarter of the cabbage mixture and drizzle with 1 to 2 tablespoons (24 to 48 g) chili-garlic sauce, as desired.

Recipe Notes

No unicorns were harmed during the preparation of these tacos!

Seitan Saag

▶ QUICK AND EASY

We admit to rarely seeing seitan on a menu at an Indian restaurant. (Okay, actually never in person.) But that wasn't about to stop us from giving it a chance. This dish might not be authentic, but it is certainly a flavorful way to get your protein. The greens are an added bonus.

1 tablespoon (15 ml) high heat neutral-flavored oil

8 ounces (227 g) Kind-to-Cows Seitan (page 138), cut into small cubes

1 cup (160 g) minced onion

2 teaspoons ground cumin

1 teaspoon ground coriander

½ teaspoon garam masala

½ teaspoon turmeric

1 tablespoon (10 g) minced garlic

2 teaspoons grated fresh ginger root

1 pound (454 g) spinach, chopped finely

3 tablespoons (45 ml) water, more if needed

1 tablespoon (16 g) tomato paste

Juice from ½ lemon, optional

Salt and pepper

YIELD: 4 servings
PROTEIN CONTENT PER SERVING: 25 g

Heat the oil in a large skillet over medium-high heat. Add the seitan and onions, and cook for 5 to 8 minutes, stirring, until the cubes are browned and the onions are softened. Reduce the heat to medium-low. Add the cumin, coriander, garam masala, and turmeric. Cook, stirring, for 2 minutes, until fragrant, to lightly toast the spices. Add the garlic, ginger, and spinach and cook for 5 to 7 minutes, stirring occasionally, until the spinach is wilted. Whisk the water and tomato paste together, and then stir into the seitan mixture. Cook for 10 minutes, stirring occasionally, for the flavors to meld. Add additional water 1 tablespoon (15 ml) at a time, if needed, to keep the mixture from sticking. Stir in the lemon juice (if using) and season to taste with salt and pepper.

Recipe Notes

• For a more traditional saag, purée the spinach in a food processor before adding.

• For Chana Saag: Omit the seitan. Add 1 can (15 ounces, or 425 g) chickpeas, drained and rinsed, along with the cumin and other spices. The rest of the recipe remains the same.

Fake-Out Take-Out Sesame Seitan with Broccoli

▶ QUICK AND EASY

It's just a little bit easier to order take-out than it is to make this dish, but making your own kicks the take-out to the curb. We like it with the sambal oelek. Feel free to omit it for a tamer dish.

1½ cups (355 ml) chilled vegetable broth, divided

3 tablespoons (45 ml) tamari

2 tablespoons (30 ml) seasoned rice vinegar

1 tablespoon (15 g) sambal oelek, or to taste, optional

1 teaspoon sriracha, or to taste

5 tablespoons (40 g) cornstarch, divided

½ teaspoon 5-spice powder

12 ounces (340 g) Kind-to-Cows Seitan (page 138), cut into bite-sized pieces, or 20 medallions

2 tablespoons (30 ml) high heat neutral-flavored oil

1 head of broccoli, cut into florets

1 teaspoon toasted sesame oil

4 cloves garlic, minced

½ teaspoon grated fresh ginger root

⅓ cup (33 g) minced scallion

2 tablespoons (16 g) toasted sesame seeds

Salt and pepper

Rice for serving, optional

YIELD: 4 servings
PROTEIN CONTENT PER SERVING: 38 g

In a small bowl, combine 1 cup (235 ml) of broth, the tamari, vinegar, sambal oelek, and sriracha. Whisk in 2 tablespoons (16 g) of cornstarch. Set aside.

Combine 3 tablespoons (24 g) of cornstarch with the 5-spice powder on a plate. Dredge the seitan pieces in the mixture. Heat the oil in a wok or large skillet over high heat. When the oil starts to ripple, reduce the heat to medium-high and add the seitan. It may spatter, so be careful. Cook the seitan for 4 to 6 minutes, stirring occasionally, until browned. Remove from the wok and set aside.

In the same wok, cook the broccoli for 3 to 4 minutes until some edges are slightly brown. Add the remaining ½ cup (120 ml) of broth and turn the heat to high. Stir and cook for 3 to 5 minutes until the broccoli is bright green and still slightly crisp. Do not overcook. Add the sesame oil, garlic, ginger, scallion, and sesame seeds. Return the seitan to the wok and pour in the sauce mixture. Cook for 3 to 5 minutes, stirring, until thickened. Season to taste and serve with rice, if desired.

Cabbage-n-Kraut with Seitan

▶ QUICK AND EASY

Adding mushrooms to this dish not only increases the protein, but also adds to the taste and texture. For a more traditional Hungarian dish, add a dollop of vegan sour cream with the garnish, if desired.

1 to 2 tablespoons (15 to 30 ml) olive oil

12 ounces (340 g) Kind-to-Cows Seitan (page 138), sliced into strips

1 medium onion, sliced

2 cups (180 g) chopped green cabbage

8 ounces (227 g) cremini mushrooms, quartered

1 teaspoon caraway seeds

1 teaspoon Hungarian paprika

1 teaspoon red pepper flakes

2 cups (284 g) drained sauerkraut

¼ cup (60 ml) dry white wine, or vegetable broth

1 tablespoon (16 g) tomato paste

1 tablespoon (8 g) nutritional yeast

8 ounces (227 g) farfalle or other flat pasta, cooked per directions (Reserve 1 cup [235 ml] cooking water.)

Juice from ½ of a lemon

Salt and pepper

¼ cup (16 g) minced fresh dill, or 1 cup (30 g) fresh spinach, minced, for garnish

YIELD: 4 servings

PROTEIN CONTENT PER SERVING: 38 g

Heat 1 tablespoon (15 ml) of oil in a large skillet over medium-high heat. Cook the seitan for 6 to 8 minutes, stirring occasionally, until browned. Remove and set aside. Reduce the heat to medium. Add the onions to the same skillet with the additional tablespoon (15 ml) of oil, if needed. Cook for 4 to 6 minutes, stirring occasionally, until softened. Add the cabbage and mushrooms, and cook for 3 to 5 minutes until the cabbage is bright green. Stir in the caraway seeds, paprika, and red pepper flakes and cook for 2 minutes. Stir in the sauerkraut.

Mix the wine or broth, tomato paste, and nutritional yeast in a small bowl. Add to the skillet, along with the seitan, and cook for 10 minutes, stirring occasionally, to meld the flavors. Stir in the pasta, and splashes of reserved cooking water, as needed, to create a saucy dish. Stir in the lemon juice, and season to taste with salt and pepper. Garnish with the dill or spinach when serving.

Mexicali Mayhem Burritos

With little hands-on time, you can have these hearty, family-pleasing burritos on the table with ease. This recipe is conservative on the heat scale with just one chipotle in adobo, but we encourage those with a passion for spicy heat to double it—or impress us by tripling it.

2 tablespoons (30 ml) olive oil, divided

4 Roma tomatoes, quartered, seeds removed

1 poblano pepper, quartered, seeds removed

½ of a small onion, cut in half, separated

3 cloves garlic, peeled

½ teaspoon fine sea salt

¼ teaspoon ground black pepper

1 chipotle in adobo, more to taste

1 tablespoon (1 g) minced fresh cilantro, or to taste

1 teaspoon apple cider vinegar, optional

12 ounces (340 g) seitan (either kind) (page 138), cut into strips

1 teaspoon ground cumin

½ teaspoon smoked paprika

4 (10-inch, or 25 cm) flour tortillas, warmed

2 cups (390 g) prepared brown rice

3 cups (110 g) shredded lettuce

2 small avocados, pitted, peeled, and sliced

YIELD: 4 burritos

PROTEIN CONTENT PER BURRITO: 44 g

Heat the oven to 400°F (200°C, or gas mark 6). Combine 1 tablespoon (15 ml) of oil, the tomatoes, poblano pepper, onion, garlic, salt, and pepper in low-rimmed baking sheet. Bake for 30 minutes, checking the garlic at 20 minutes to be sure it isn't burning. If it is, remove it and return the other vegetables to the oven until the skins on the tomatoes are wrinkled and parts of the poblano pepper are blackened. Bake for an additional 10 to 15 minutes, if needed. Transfer all the roasted ingredients into a small food processor or blender, along with the chipotle, and process until smooth. Stir in the cilantro and taste, adding the vinegar and adjusting the seasonings, if needed.

Heat the remaining tablespoon (15 ml) of oil in large skillet over medium-high heat. Toss the seitan with the cumin and smoked paprika. Cook for 4 to 6 minutes, stirring occasionally, until browned. Add the puréed vegetable sauce. Reduce the heat to low. Cook for 3 to 5 minutes, stirring occasionally, until heated throughout.

To serve, spoon ½ cup (97 g) of brown rice down the center of each burrito, leaving some space on the ends for easier rolling. Layer with one-quarter of the seitan, lettuce, and avocado. Fold the ends in and roll the burrito up to close.

Recipe Notes

• Make a burrito bar and let each person pile on the extras of their choice. Include vegan sour cream, salsa, diced tomatoes, chopped jalapeños, vegan shredded cheddar cheese, and other favorites.

• If desired, the burritos and rice can be omitted. Instead, serve the seitan mixture and any toppings over any grain of choice, such as quinoa.

Harissa Seitan and Green Beans

▶ QUICK AND EASY ▶ SOY-FREE POTENTIAL

Did you have a busy day? Or a bad day? Turn that frown upside down with this super-fast, super-flavorful dinner. It's so easy, and so good! We like to serve this over couscous, either regular whole wheat or Israeli.

1 tablespoon (15 ml) high heat neutral-flavored oil

8 ounces (227 g) Quit-the-Cluck Seitan (page 138), cut into ½-inch (1.3 cm) strips

2 handfuls green beans, trimmed, cut into bite-size pieces

½ of a red bell pepper, cut into thin strips

1 leek, white part only, cut in half, sliced into half-rounds

⅓ cup (80 ml) dry red wine, or vegetable broth

1½ tablespoons (24 g) harissa paste, or to taste

3 tablespoons (48 g) tomato paste

1 cup (235 ml) vegetable broth

2 cloves garlic, minced

Juice from ½ lemon

Salt and pepper

YIELD: 4 servings
PROTEIN CONTENT PER SERVING: 16 g

Heat the oil in a large skillet over medium-high heat. Cook the seitan for 4 to 6 minutes, stirring occasionally, until browned. Add the green beans and cook for 3 minutes until bright green. Add the bell pepper and leek, and cook, stirring, for 2 minutes, until tender but not soft. Add the ⅓ cup (75 ml) wine or broth to the skillet, scraping any bits from the bottom. Reduce the heat to medium-low. Add the harissa paste, tomato paste, broth, garlic, and lemon juice. Stir to coat the seitan and vegetables. Cook for 10 minutes, stirring occasionally. Season to taste with salt and pepper.

Barbecued Seitan

This sauce has become our go-to when we are looking for true Southern barbecue sauce. Here we serve it with seitan, but it is also wonderful on grilled tofu, tempeh, and portobellos. Pick your protein!

FOR THE SAUCE:

1 tablespoon (15 ml) olive oil, divided

⅓ cup (53 g) chopped onion

3 cloves garlic, chopped

1 can (15 ounces, or 425 g) tomato sauce

1 can (6 ounces, or 170 g) tomato paste

⅓ cup plus 1 tablespoon (90 g) packed brown sugar

2 to 3 tablespoons (40 to 60 g) molasses

2 tablespoons (30 ml) vegan Worcestershire sauce

1 tablespoon plus 1 teaspoon (20 ml) liquid smoke

1 tablespoon (8 g) chili powder

1 tablespoon (15 g) Dijon mustard

1 teaspoon fine sea salt

½ teaspoon ground black pepper

½ to 1 teaspoon cayenne pepper, or to taste

FOR THE SANDWICHES:

4 seitan cutlets, (either kind) (page 138)

1 tablespoon (15 ml) olive oil

½ of a small onion, thinly sliced

½ of a small bell pepper (any color), thinly sliced

4 burger buns or crusty rolls, split and toasted

2 tablespoons (28 g) vegan mayonnaise, optional

YIELD: 4 sandwiches, plus 2½ cups (625 g) sauce

PROTEIN CONTENT PER SANDWICH (WITH SAUCE): 34 g

To make the sauce: Heat 1 tablespoon (15 ml) of oil in a medium-size saucepan over medium heat. Add the onion and cook for 5 minutes, stirring occasionally, until translucent. Add the garlic and cook for 1 minute. Add the tomato sauce through the cayenne pepper, stirring well to combine. Bring to a boil, and then reduce the heat to a simmer. Cook for 30 minutes, stirring occasionally. The sauce should be thick enough to leave trails in the surface. For a thicker sauce, cook longer. Transfer the sauce to a blender and process until smooth.

To make the sandwiches: Slice the cutlets into thin strips. Heat the oil in a large skillet over medium-high heat. Cook the seitan for 6 to 8 minutes, stirring occasionally, until browned. Add the onion and bell pepper and cook for 2 minutes, so the pepper remains slightly crisp. Reduce the heat to low and add the sauce, as desired. Cook for 3 minutes to combine and heat throughout. Spread the mayonnaise evenly on the bottom buns. Divide the mixture on the buns and put the tops on. Extra sauce can be refrigerated for up to 1 week or frozen for up to 2 months.

Snow Storm Seitan and Root Stew

The aroma of this classic stew simmering on the stove will have your family circling the kitchen in anticipation. It's a sure cure for the winter blahs.

12 ounces (340 g) Kind-to-Cows Seitan (page 138)

3 tablespoons (23 g) all-purpose flour

3 tablespoons (45 ml) high heat neutral-flavored oil, divided

4 ounces (113 g) cremini mushrooms, quartered

⅔ cup (81 g) 1-inch (2.5 cm) pieces of carrot

½ of a medium onion, cut into 1-inch (2.5 cm) pieces

½ cup (50 g) ½-inch (1.3 cm) pieces celery

½ cup (55 g) 1-inch (2.5 cm) pieces parsnip

½ cup (70 g) 1-inch (2.5 cm) pieces turnip

5 shiitake caps, cut in slivers

3 cloves garlic, minced

1 dried bay leaf

¼ teaspoon paprika

¼ teaspoons dried ground rosemary

¼ teaspoon dried thyme

¼ cup (60 ml) dry red wine, or additional broth

2 cups (470 ml) vegetable broth

Salt and pepper

8 ounces (227 g) fingerling potatoes, roasted (See Recipe Notes.)

YIELD: 4 servings
PROTEIN CONTENT PER SERVING: 37 g

Cut the seitan into 1-inch (2.5 cm) pieces. Combine the flour, salt, and pepper on a plate. Add the seitan, coating it well. Heat 2 tablespoons (30 ml) of oil in a large pot over medium heat. Add the seitan, scraping in the excess flour and seasonings. Cook for 7 to 9 minutes, stirring occasionally, until the seitan is browned. Add the remaining tablespoon (15 ml) of oil and the mushrooms through the thyme. Cook for 4 to 6 minutes, stirring, until the vegetables are glazed. Reduce the heat if the garlic starts to brown. Add the ¼ cup (60 ml) wine or broth, scraping any bits from the bottom, and cook for 3 to 4 minutes. Add the 2 cups (470 ml) broth, bring to a boil, and then reduce the heat to a simmer. Cook for 30 minutes. Stir in the roasted fingerlings. Cook for 10 minutes or until the root vegetables are tender. Remove the bay leaf. Taste and adjust the seasonings.

Recipe Notes

• To roast fingerlings: Preheat the oven to 400°F (200°C, or gas mark 6). Cut 8 ounces (227 g) of fingerling potatoes into ½-inch (1.3 cm) rounds. Toss with 1 tablespoon (15 ml) olive oil and season with salt and pepper. Bake for 20 to 30 minutes until the potatoes are tender.

• Just can't get enough vegetables? Add ½ cup (50 g) 1-inch (2.5 cm) pieces green beans or ½ cup (75 g) peas along with the fingerling potatoes, or both.

Jumbo Pot O'Gumbo

Hats off to the awesome HBO series *Treme* for making gumbo sound so irresistible, we just had to make our own.

½ cup (60 g) whole wheat flour

3 tablespoons (45 ml) neutral-flavored oil, divided

2 Smoky Sausages (page 140), chopped into bite-size pieces

¼ cup (60 ml) water, plus more as needed

1 medium onion, chopped

1½ cups (150 g) chopped celery

1 green bell pepper, trimmed and chopped (about 8 ounces, or 227 g)

4 cloves garlic, grated or pressed

1 teaspoon smoked or regular paprika

½ teaspoon fine sea salt, or to taste

½ teaspoon garlic powder

½ teaspoon onion powder

½ teaspoon dried oregano

½ teaspoon dried thyme

¼ teaspoon cayenne pepper

Ground black pepper

2 tablespoons (33 g) tomato paste

2 tablespoons (30 ml) vegan Worcestershire sauce

1 dried bay leaf

4 cups (940 ml) vegetable broth

4½ to 6 cups (878 to 1170 g) cooked long-grain brown rice

Hot sauce, to taste

2 to 3 tablespoons (8 to 11 g) chopped fresh parsley

YIELD: 8 servings
PROTEIN CONTENT PER SERVING: 26 g

Preheat the oven to 375° F (190° C or gas mark 5). Add the flour to an oven-safe skillet, spreading it evenly. Stir frequently, making sure not to miss the edges so the flour won't scorch. Cook until medium-dark brown, about 30 minutes. Set aside. Sift the flour once cooled.

In a large pot, heat 2 tablespoons (30 ml) of oil over medium-high heat. Add the sausage and cook until browned, about 6 minutes. Remove the sausage and set aside. Deglaze the pan with ¼ cup (60 ml) water, stirring to detach the browned bits at the bottom of the pan, and transfer this mixture to a measuring cup, adding enough water to reach a total of ½ cup (120 ml) of liquid. Set aside.

Add the remaining tablespoon (15 ml) of oil to the pot. Add the onion, celery, bell pepper, garlic, paprika, salt, garlic powder, onion powder, oregano, thyme, cayenne pepper, and black pepper and cook until the vegetables just start to get tender, about 6 minutes.

Whisk the deglazing liquid with browned flour until a smooth paste forms. Add the tomato paste and Worcestershire sauce, stirring until combined.

Add the sausage, browned flour mixture, bay leaf, and broth to the vegetables. Bring to a boil. Lower the heat, cover with a lid, and simmer for 1 hour, stirring occasionally.

Remove the pot from the heat. Discard the bay leaf. Divide the rice and ladle the gumbo on each portion. Garnish with hot sauce to taste, and chopped parsley.

Leftovers can be stored in an airtight container in the refrigerator for up to 4 days or frozen for up to 3 months.

White Chili

▶ SOY-FREE POTENTIAL

This satisfying stick-to-your-ribs chili is made without a tomato in sight. Tomatillos, originally from Mexico, add a tang to this hearty dish.

1 tablespoon (15 ml) olive oil

8 ounces (227 g) Quit-the-Cluck Seitan (page 138), cut into bite-size pieces

1 cup (160 g) chopped onion

4 cloves garlic, minced

2 to 3 small white potatoes (180 g), chopped into small cubes

4 ounces (113 g) mushrooms (any kind), quartered

1 poblano pepper, seeded and chopped

1 jalapeño pepper, seeded and minced

3 tomatillos, husks removed, chopped

2 teaspoons ground cumin

1 teaspoon dried oregano

1 teaspoon dried thyme

1 teaspoon chili powder

½ teaspoon dried cilantro

¼ teaspoon ground black pepper

1 can (15 ounces, or 425 g) Great Northern beans, drained and rinsed

½ cup (82 g) frozen corn, (run under hot water, drained)

2 cups (470 ml) vegetable broth, more if needed (See Recipe Note.)

Salt and pepper

YIELD: 4 servings

PROTEIN CONTENT PER SERVING: 28 grams

Heat the oil in a large soup pot over medium heat. Add the seitan and onion and cook for 5 minutes, stirring occasionally, until the onion is translucent. Add the garlic, potatoes, mushrooms, peppers, tomatillos, cumin, oregano, thyme, chili powder, cilantro, and black pepper. Cook for 3 to 4 minutes, stirring, until fragrant. Add the beans, corn, and broth. Bring to a boil, and then reduce the heat to a simmer. The ingredients should be covered by the broth. If not, add broth as needed. Cook for 30 to 45 minutes, stirring occasionally, until the potatoes are tender. Taste and adjust the seasonings.

Recipe Note

The amount of broth needed will depend on the type of pot used. Have extra broth on hand, just in case.

Cock-a-Leekie Stew with Roasted Asparagus

▶ SOY-FREE POTENTIAL

Known as the national soup of Scotland, our stew version is brimming with leeks. Quit-the-Cluck Seitan stands in for the chicken. Our cruelty-free version is superior to the original in many ways. One of the most important ways is in what it doesn't have: cholesterol, like all plant-based foods. Oh, and it tastes amazing, too.

1 tablespoon (15 ml) high heat neutral-flavored oil

8 ounces (227 g) Quit-the-Cluck Seitan (page 138), cut into bite-size pieces

4 ounces (113 g) cremini mushrooms, minced

1 teaspoon fine sea salt

1 teaspoon liquid smoke

5 cups (1 pound, or 454 g) white part only, sliced leeks

1 stalk celery, diced

1 large carrot, diced

1 medium russet potato, shredded

½ cup (120 ml) dry white wine, or vegetable broth

3 cloves garlic, minced

2 tablespoons (15 g) nutritional yeast

1 bouquet garni (See Recipe Notes.)

2 teaspoons dried poultry seasoning

½ teaspoon dried thyme

½ teaspoon dried tarragon

1 teaspoon ground white pepper

½ cup (100 g) dry pearl barley

4 to 5 cups (940 ml to 1.2 L) vegetable broth

12 ounces (340 g) asparagus, cut into 1-inch (2.5 cm) pieces, roasted

Minced fresh parsley, for garnish

YIELD: 4 servings

PROTEIN CONTENT PER SERVING: 22 g

Heat the oil in a large soup pot over medium-high heat. Add the seitan and cook for 4 to 6 minutes, stirring occasionally, until browned. Remove and set aside. To the same pot, add the mushrooms and salt. Cook for 3 to 4 minutes until soft. Reduce the heat to medium. Stir in the liquid smoke. Add the leeks, celery, carrot, and potato and cook for 6 to 8 minutes, stirring occasionally, until the leeks are softened. Add the ½ cup (120 ml) wine or broth through the barley and the reserved seitan. Cook until the liquid is evaporated or absorbed, scraping any bits from the bottom. Add 4 cups (940 ml) of broth, bring to a boil, and then reduce the heat to a simmer. Simmer for 1 hour, uncovered, until the barley is done. Stir occasionally and add additional broth, if desired. Remove the bouquet garni. Serve each portion topped with one-quarter of the asparagus and sprinkled with parsley.

Recipe Notes

• Bouquet garni is a fancy term which means to wrap a couple twigs of fresh thyme, rosemary, and a dried bay leaf in a piece of cheesecloth. Tie it closed.

• To roast asparagus: Preheat the oven to 400°F (200°C, or gas mark 6). Toss the asparagus with 1 tablespoon (15 ml) olive oil. Season with salt and pepper. Bake for 12 to 15 minutes, or to desired tenderness.

Roasted Seitan, Potatoes, and Garlic

This hearty "meat" and potatoes dish only needs a lush green salad or a bright green vegetable to make a quick traditional-style meal. Using both fresh and dry herbs adds layers of flavor.

Nonstick cooking spray

¼ cup (32 g) all-purpose flour

1 teaspoon dried thyme

½ teaspoon dried rosemary

4 (each 4 ounce, or 113 g) Quit-the-Cluck Seitan cutlets (page 138)

1 tablespoon (15 ml) high heat neutral-flavored oil

1½ pounds (680 g) small yellow or red potatoes, cut into 1-inch (2.5 cm) cubes

40 cloves garlic, peeled, sliced vertically in half

1½ tablespoons (12 g) nutritional yeast

1½ teaspoons sweet paprika

½ teaspoon fine sea salt

¼ teaspoon ground black pepper

1 teaspoon minced fresh rosemary, more for garnish

1 teaspoon minced fresh thyme

¾ cup (180 ml) vegetable broth

¼ cup (60 ml) dry white wine, or additional broth

1 tablespoon (15 ml) fresh lemon juice

YIELD: 4 servings

PROTEIN CONTENT PER SERVING: 35 g

Preheat the oven to 400°F (200°C, or gas mark 6). Spray a 9 x 13 inch (22 x 33 cm) deep baking dish with cooking spray.

Combine the flour, dried thyme, dried rosemary, and a pinch of salt and pepper on a plate. Lightly coat the seitan cutlets with the flour mixture. Heat the oil in a large skillet over medium-high heat. Cook the cutlets for 3 to 5 minutes until browned. Turn over and cook the second side for 3 to 4 minutes until also browned. Transfer the cutlets to the baking dish.

Put the remaining salt, potatoes, garlic, nutritional yeast, spices, seasonings, and herbs in a large bowl, stirring to coat. Spread around and on top of the cutlets in the baking dish. Pour the broth and ¼ cup (60 ml) wine or additional broth over the seitan and potatoes. To ensure the garlic bakes, be sure it is submerged. Bake for 50 minutes, until the potatoes are tender. Carefully stir the potatoes after the first 30 minutes, tucking the garlic into the broth.

To serve, put a cutlet on each plate. Pour the lemon juice into the potatoes. Stir to combine and adjust the seasonings. Spoon the potatoes evenly onto the plates and garnish with fresh rosemary.

Seitan Marsala

▶ SOY-FREE POTENTIAL

This is easy to make—as Marsala always is—but a few extra touches take this comfort dish to a new, modern place. Serve over mashed potatoes, pasta, or even rice.

¼ cup (32 g) all-purpose flour, plus 3 tablespoons (24 g), divided

Pinch of fine sea salt

Pinch of ground black pepper

4 (each 4 ounces, or 113 g) Quit-the-Cluck Seitan cutlets (page 138)

3 tablespoons (45 ml) olive oil

¾ cup (120 g) minced shallot

¼ plus cup 2 tablespoons (54 g) minced bell pepper (any color)

12 ounces (340 g) cremini mushrooms, sliced

6 sun-dried tomato halves (moist vacuum-packed), thinly sliced

5 cloves garlic, thinly sliced

¾ teaspoon dried thyme, or 2½ teaspoons minced fresh thyme

Pinch of dried tarragon

½ cup (120 ml) vegan Marsala wine

1 cup (235 ml) vegetable broth, more if needed

Salt and pepper

Fresh minced parsley, for garnish

YIELD: 4 servings
PROTEIN CONTENT PER SERVING: 32 g

Preheat the oven to 300°F (150°C, or gas mark 2).

Combine ¼ cup (32 g) flour with a pinch of salt and pepper on a plate. Dredge both sides of the cutlets in the flour mixture. Heat 2 tablespoons (30 ml) of oil in a large skillet over medium-high heat. Cook the cutlets for 3 to 5 minutes until browned. Turn over to cook the second side for 3 to 4 minutes until also browned. Keep warm in the oven.

Reduce the heat to medium. Add the remaining tablespoon (15 ml) oil, shallot, bell pepper, and the remaining 3 tablespoons (24 g) flour to the same skillet. Cook and stir for 3 to 5 minutes until the shallot is softened.

Add the mushrooms, sun-dried tomatoes, garlic, thyme, and tarragon. Cook for 4 to 6 minutes until the mushrooms darken slightly. Add the wine and broth and bring to a simmer. Cook for 15 minutes. Add additional broth to thin the sauce, if desired. Taste and adjust the seasonings.

Put the cutlets into the skillet and spoon some of the sauce on top. For best texture contrast, do not cover the cutlets completely with the sauce. Garnish with the parsley.

Easy Seitan for Two

▶ QUICK AND EASY

Pull the seitan out of the freezer, and this dish can be on the table in minutes. We like to match it with mashed potatoes and a green vegetable. With such a simple recipe, you'll be surprised how satisfying this protein and potato dinner is.

½ teaspoon freshly ground black pepper

Pinch of fine sea salt

2 (each 4 ounces, or 113 g) Kind-to-Cows Seitan cutlets (page 138)

⅓ cup (80 ml) vegetable broth

1 tablespoon (16 g) tomato paste

1 teaspoon balsamic vinegar

1 teaspoon Dijon mustard

1 teaspoon white miso

1 tablespoon (15 ml) high heat neutral-flavored oil

2 tablespoons (20 g) minced shallot

YIELD: 2 servings

PROTEIN CONTENT PER SERVING: 43 g

Rub the pepper and salt evenly into the seitan cutlets.

Whisk together the broth, tomato paste, vinegar, mustard, and miso in a small bowl.

Heat the oil over medium-high heat in a large skillet. Put the cutlets into the skillet and cook for 3 to 5 minutes, until browned. Turn over and cook the second side for 3 to 4 minutes until also browned. Remove the cutlets and set aside.

Reduce the heat to medium-low. Add the shallots. Cook and stir for 2 to 3 minutes, until softened. Be careful not to burn them. Scrape up any bits stuck to the skillet. Pour the broth mixture into the skillet. Bring to a simmer and stir for 3 to 4 minutes. Put the cutlets back into the skillet and turn to coat. Simmer for 3 to 4 minutes to heat the cutlets throughout. Spoon the sauce over the cutlets to serve.

Pecan-Crusted Seitan Cutlets with Brussels Sprouts

Who says protein can't be romantic? Not us! The delightful crunch brings a sensational texture to the cutlets, while the Brussels sprouts, well, they're perfect any time. Try this recipe for your next date night . . . may the sparks fly!

FOR THE CUTLETS:

½ cup (120 ml) unsweetened plain vegan milk

3 tablespoons (42 g) vegan mayonnaise

1 tablespoon (15 g) Dijon mustard

¼ teaspoon fine sea salt, plus a pinch

⅛ teaspoon ground black pepper, plus a pinch

½ cup plus 2 tablespoons (63 g) pecan halves, ground

3 tablespoons (15 g) panko crumbs

1½ teaspoons onion powder

2 (each 4 ounces, or 113 g) Kind-to-Cows Seitan cutlets (page 138)

High heat neutral-flavored oil, for cooking

FOR THE BRUSSELS SPROUTS:

1 tablespoon (15 ml) olive oil

12 ounces (340 g) Brussels sprouts, very thinly sliced

2 tablespoons (30 ml) vegetable broth

1 teaspoon Dijon mustard

3 tablespoons (21 g) grated carrots

Salt and pepper

YIELD: 2 servings

PROTEIN CONTENT PER SERVING: 51 g

To make the cutlets: Whisk together the milk, mayonnaise, mustard, and a pinch each of salt and pepper in a shallow bowl. Combine the pecans, panko, onion powder, and remaining salt and pepper on a plate. Stir to combine. Line a baking sheet with parchment paper. Using one "wet" hand and one "dry" hand, dip each cutlet in the milk mixture, then in the pecan mixture, turning to coat well. Put on the lined baking sheet and repeat with the second cutlet. Refrigerate for 15 minutes or up to 8 hours. This helps to set the coating so it will not fall off during cooking.

To cook the cutlets, heat a thin layer of oil in a large heavy-bottomed skillet. Cook the cutlets for 5 to 7 minutes until browned. Turn over and cook the second side for 4 to 6 minutes until also browned.

To make the Brussels sprouts: Heat the oil in a large skillet over medium-high heat. Add the Brussels sprouts. Cook for 6 to 8 minutes, stirring occasionally. The Brussels sprouts should have some dark spots and be tender. Whisk together the broth and mustard in a small bowl. Turn the heat off, but leave the skillet on the heat. Stir in the broth mixture and the carrots. The liquid should evaporate or be absorbed. Season to taste with salt and pepper.

To serve, divide the Brussels sprouts on two plates and top each with a cutlet.

Seitan Paprikash

Yet another classic protein dish takes the leap into being vegan! This full-flavor sauce perfectly coats the seitan and the slightly crisp vegetables.

1 cup (235 ml) water

¼ cup (35 g) raw cashews

1½ cups (355 ml) vegetable broth, divided

1 tablespoon (15 ml) apple cider vinegar

1 tablespoon (15 ml) unsweetened plain vegan milk

1½ teaspoons fresh lemon juice

Salt and pepper

⅓ cup plus 1 tablespoon (50 g) all-purpose flour

3 (each 4 ounces, or 113 g) Quit-the-Cluck Seitan cutlets (page 138), cut into quarters, or 12 nuggets (page 144)

2 tablespoons (30 ml) high heat neutral-flavored oil

1 medium onion, cut into ½-inch (1.3 cm) thick slices

1 red bell pepper, cut into ¼-inch (6 mm) thick slices

4 cloves garlic, minced

2 tablespoons (14 g) Hungarian paprika

½ teaspoon caraway seeds, optional

3 tablespoons (48 g) tomato paste

Bring the water to a boil in small saucepan. Add the cashews. Reduce the heat to a simmer and cook for 10 minutes. Drain and transfer to a small high-powered blender and add ¼ cup (60 ml) of broth, vinegar, milk, lemon juice, and a pinch of salt. Process until completely smooth and set aside.

Combine the flour with a pinch of salt and pepper on a shallow plate. Dredge the seitan in the flour to cover completely. Heat the oil in a large skillet over medium-high heat. Cook the seitan (in batches) for 4 to 6 minutes, until browned. Turn over and cook the second side for 3 to 5 minutes until also browned. Remove and set aside.

Reduce the heat to medium. Add the onions to the same skillet, scraping any bits from the bottom. Cook for 4 to 6 minutes until softened. Add the bell pepper and cook for 3 to 4 minutes. The pepper should still have some crunch. Add the garlic, paprika, and caraway seeds, and cook and stir for 2 minutes. Add the remaining 1¼ cups (295 ml) broth, and tomato paste. Bring to a boil, then reduce the heat to a simmer for 10 to 12 minutes, or until thickened. Add the cashew mixture, stirring to combine. Add the seitan pieces and simmer for 4 to 6 minutes until heated throughout. Taste and adjust the seasonings. Serve over pasta or a grain, if desired.

YIELD: 4 servings

PROTEIN CONTENT PER SERVING: 27 g

Braciola

We couldn't resist recreating this Italian masterpiece. Rather than the traditional meat, we use seitan cutlets. Our pesto-like filling and luscious red pepper sauce are unique twists on the original. We know, it sounds like a restaurant-style meal. But trust us, it's easier to make than you think!

FOR THE SAUCE:

1 tablespoon (15 ml) olive oil

½ cup (80 g) minced shallot

3 cloves garlic, minced

½ cup plus 1 tablespoon (101 g) jarred roasted red peppers, rinsed, drained, and chopped

1 can (14.5 ounces, or 411 g) diced tomatoes, drained

½ teaspoon dried red pepper flakes

½ teaspoon dried Italian seasoning blend

¼ cup (60 ml) dry red wine, or vegetable broth

Salt and pepper

FOR THE BRACIOLA:

¾ ounce (23 g) fresh basil

Handful baby spinach

2 tablespoons (18 g) pine nuts

4 sun-dried tomato halves (moist vacuum-packed)

1 tablespoon (8 g) nutritional yeast

2 cloves garlic, minced

2 teaspoons fresh lemon juice

1 cup (50 g) fresh bread crumbs

Salt and pepper

2 Kind-to-Cows Seitan cutlets (page 138), made braciola-style

1 tablespoon (15 ml) olive oil, for cooking

YIELD: 4 servings
PROTEIN CONTENT PER SERVING: 68 g

To make the sauce: Heat the olive oil in a medium-size saucepan over medium-high heat. Add the shallot and cook for 3 to 4 minutes, until soft. Add the garlic through the wine or broth. Bring to a boil, and then reduce the heat to a simmer. Cook for 15 minutes. Blend the sauce until smooth using an immersion blender or blender. Season to taste.

To make the braciola: Combine the basil through the lemon juice in a food processor. Process until pasty. Stir in the bread crumbs and season to taste with salt and pepper. Lay the cutlets on a work surface with the 8-inch (20 cm) side parallel to your body. Put one-half of the filling (½ cup, or 50 g) about 1-inch (2.5 cm) up from the edge closest to your body. Shape the filling into a roll, not quite extending to the edges of the cutlet. Cut 6 12-inch (30 cm) pieces of cooking twine. Carefully roll the cutlet around the filling and up the cutting board, repacking any filling that falls out. Tie the middle and ends of each roll, using 3 pieces of twine on each.

Heat the oil in a large skillet over medium-high heat. Put the rolls into the skillet. Sear each side, for 3 to 4 minutes. The rolls are prone to sticking, so use a spatula to gently turn them. Pour the sauce over the rolls and cook on medium-low for 5 minutes.

Remove the rolls from the sauce and use toothpicks to secure the roll every inch (2.5 cm). Slice into 1-inch (2.5 cm) rounds. Serve over pasta or a grain, if desired. Spoon the sauce over the slices.

Seitan Bolognese

Traditionally, this sauce is all about the meat. Swapping in seitan is an easy-peasy recipe fix. That's a good start, but we vegans wanted more vegetables, too! Is it historically accurate? No. But we think it's better, and certainly cruelty-free. Please note: Before draining the noodles, scoop out 1 cup (235 ml) of the cooking water.

12 ounces (340 g) Kind-to-Cows Seitan cutlets (page 138)

2 tablespoons (30 ml) olive oil

½ cup (80 g) minced onion

¼ cup (28 g) minced carrot

¼ cup (36 g) minced green bell pepper

3 tablespoons (22 g) minced celery

4 ounces (113 g) cremini mushrooms, minced

1 tablespoon (10 g) minced garlic

½ teaspoon dried thyme, or 1½ teaspoons fresh

½ teaspoon red pepper flakes

1 bay leaf

Pinch of grated nutmeg

⅔ cup (160 ml) dry white wine, or vegetable broth

1 can (14.5 ounces, or 411 g) diced fire-roasted tomatoes, undrained

3 tablespoons (45 ml) vegetable broth

2 tablespoons (32 g) tomato paste

1 vegetable bouillon cube

¾ cup (180 ml) unsweetened soymilk

Salt and pepper

12 ounces (340 g) flat, wide noodles, cooked (See headnote.)

YIELD: 4 servings

PROTEIN CONTENT PER SERVING: 47 g

Tear the seitan cutlets into large pieces. Use a food processor to pulse the pieces into chunks. Try not to process the seitan into a mince, but leave various sizes of chunks from 1-inch (2.5 cm) to smaller. Heat the oil in a large pot over medium-high heat. Add the seitan and cook for 4 to 6 minutes, stirring occasionally, until browned. Some of the seitan will stick to the pot, and that is alright. Add the onion through the nutmeg and cook, stirring for 3 to 5 minutes, until the onion is translucent.

Reduce the heat to medium. Add the ⅔ cup (160 ml) wine or broth, scraping any bits from the bottom. Add the tomatoes, 3 tablespoons (45 ml) vegetable broth, tomato paste, and bouillon cube. Lower the heat and simmer the sauce for one hour. While simmering, stir in ¼ cup (60 ml) of soymilk at a time every 15 minutes until all the soymilk is added. Stir occasionally while cooking. Remove the bay leaf and season to taste. Add the noodles to the pot and stir to coat, adding up to 1 cup (235 ml) cooking water if needed to make the mixture saucier.

Home-Style Potpie

If you grew up with a vegan mom cooking for you, you'd be writing this recipe, not us. We think this is going to be a favorite in your home. Hearty vegetables and seitan are cooked in a rich, mushroom gravy. You can make this potpie with a single crust, or a double, whichever you prefer.

¼ cup plus 2 tablespoons (47 g) all-purpose flour, divided

12 ounces (340 g) Quit-the-Cluck Seitan, cut into 1-inch (2.5 cm) pieces

3 tablespoons (45 ml) neutral-flavored oil, divided

4 ounces (113 g) cremini mushrooms, finely minced

1 cup (160 g) diced onion

1 cup (110 g) diced yellow or red potatoes

¾ cup (98 g) diced carrot

½ cup (55 g) diced parsnip

¼ cup (30 g) diced celery

1 teaspoon dried thyme

1 teaspoon dried poultry seasoning

3 cloves garlic, minced

2 tablespoons (15 g) nutritional yeast

1½ cups (355 ml) vegetable broth

⅓ cup (43 g) frozen peas (run under hot water, drained)

1 tablespoon (15 ml) tamari

Salt and pepper

Single or double non-sweet pie crust recipe, or store-bought

YIELD: 1 (8-inch, or 20 cm) potpie
PROTEIN CONTENT PER SERVING: 47 g

Preheat the oven to 375°F (190°C, or gas mark 5).

Combine ¼ cup (31 g) of flour and a pinch of salt and pepper in a shallow dish. Add the seitan, tossing to coat. Heat 2 tablespoons (30 ml) of oil in a large skillet over medium-high heat. Add the seitan and cook for 5 minutes, stirring occasionally, until browned. Remove from the skillet and set aside. Add the remaining table-spoon (15 ml) oil and the mushrooms through the celery and ½ teaspoon salt to the same skillet. Reduce the heat to medium and cook for 8 to 10 minutes, stirring occasionally. The vegetables will soften and lose their brightness. Add the thyme through the nutritional yeast and remaining 2 tablespoons (16 g) flour. Cook for 3 to 4 minutes, stirring, to cook the flour. Add the reserved seitan, broth, peas, and tamari, scraping any bits from the bottom. Stir to combine, and cook for 5 minutes, until thickened. Season to taste with salt and pepper.

If using a double crust, line an 8-inch (20 cm) pie plate with the crust. Spoon the filling into the crust. (Alternatively, if using one crust, pour the filling into the pie plate.)

Crimp and seal the dough along the rim of the pie plate. Make a few cuts to let the steam escape. (Alternatively, use a cutter to cut out pieces of the dough and decoratively cover the filling, letting each piece overlap.) Place a baking sheet in the oven in case the potpie cooks over and put the potpie on top of it. Bake for 35 to 40 minutes until the filling is bubbly.

Acknowledgments

Many thanks to Amanda Waddell, Betsy Gammons, Heather Godin, Katie Fawkes, and Jenna Patton for making the whole cookbook-writing experience completely awesome, without fail. A big thank you to Anya Todd, for reviewing the nutrition data in this book.

Our testers take the cake (vegan, that is), time and time again! Thanks to Courtney Blair, Kelly and Mac Cavalier, Michelle Cavigliano, Shannon Davis, Zsu Dever, Dorian Farrow, Monique and Michel Narbel-Gimzia, Jenna Patton, Constanze Reichardt, Stephanie Bly Sulzman, and Liz Wyman.

Tami thanks Jim (always!), her family, and her Cle-Vegan friends. Big thanks to Celine, of course.

Celine says *merci beaucoup* to Mamou, Papou, Chaz, and Tami.

About the Authors

Celine Steen is the coauthor of *500 Vegan Recipes*, *The Complete Guide to Vegan Food Substitutions*, *Hearty Vegan Meals for Monster Appetites*, *Vegan Sandwiches Save the Day!*, *Whole Grain Vegan Baking*, and *Vegan Finger Foods*. She blogs at www.havecakewilltravel.com. You can contact her at celine@havecakewilltravel.com.

Tami Noyes is the author of *American Vegan Kitchen* and *Grills Gone Vegan* and the coauthor of *Vegan Sandwiches Save the Day!*, *Whole Grain Vegan Baking*, and *Vegan Finger Foods*. She lives, cooks, and blogs in her five-kitty home in Ohio. Follow her blog at www.veganappetite.com, or e-mail Tami at veganappetite@gmail.com.

Index